Francis of Assisi's
Canticle of the Creatures

Saint Francis to the Birds

Up soared the lark into the air,
A shaft of song, a winged prayer,
As if a soul, released from pain,
Were flying back to heaven again.

St. Francis heard; it was to him
An emblem of the Seraphim;
The upward motion of the fire,
The light, the heat, the heart's desire.

Around Assisi's convent gate
The birds, God's poor who cannot wait,
From moor and mere and dark-some wood
Came flocking for their dole of food.

"O brother birds," St. Francis said,
"Ye come to me and ask for bread,
But not with bread alone to-day
Shall ye be fed and sent away.

"Ye shall be fed, ye happy birds,
With manna of celestial words;
Not mine, though mine they seem to be,
Not mine, though they be spoke through me.

"O, doubly are ye bound to praise
The great Creator in your lays;
He giveth you your plumes of down,
Your crimson hoods, your cloaks of brown.

"He giveth you your wings to fly
And breathe a purer air on high,
And careth for you everywhere,
Who for yourselves so little care!"

With flutter of swift wings and songs
Together rose the feathered throngs,
And singing scattered far apart;
Deep peace was in St. Francis' heart.

He knew not if the brotherhood
His homily had understood;
He only knew that to one ear
The meaning of his words was clear.

—Henry Wadsworth Longfellow

Francis of Assisi's Canticle of the Creatures

A MODERN SPIRITUAL PATH

PAUL M. ALLEN

AND

JOAN deRIS ALLEN

CONTINUUM · NEW YORK

1996
The Continuum Publishing Company
370 Lexington Avenue
New York, NY 10017

Printed in the United States of America
Library of Congress Cataloging-in- Publication Data
Allen, Paul Marshall.
    Francis of Assisi's canticle of the creatures : a modern
spiritual path / Paul M. Allen and Joan deRis Allen.
    p.   cm.
Includes bibliographical references.
ISBN 0-8264-0876-1 (alk. paper)
1. Francis, of Assisi, Saint, 1182–1226.   Cantico di frate sole.
2. Nature—Religious aspects—Christianity.   3. Spirituality.
4. Hymns, Italian.   I. Allen, Joan deRis, 1931– .   II. Title.
BV489.F74C363 1996
242'.721—dc20   95-44574
                                                                CIP

Contents

Illustrations

Note to the Reader

While to a certain extent it is hoped that this book will give the reader an introduction to the life story of Francis of Assisi, it is not primarily intended to be a biography of the man. This later task has already been amply fulfilled by a host of writers throughout the centuries since Francis's time, beginning with the outstanding accounts by Thomas of Celano, St. Bonaventure, and others. Although we have drawn liberally from these sources, we are most of all indebted to the monumental biography by the late Arnaldo Fortini, *Nova Vita di San Francesco* (Tipografia Porziuncola, Santa Maria degli Angeli, 1959) and particularly to the English translation of a part of it by Helen Moak (Crossroad Publishing Co., New York, 1981). The Italian original of this work reflects not only a lifetime of painstaking historical research, but in itself brings something of the poetic warmth and humaneness so characteristic of the biographer, as well as of Francis himself.

The second major source of great help in preparing this volume is *Francis of Assisi, An Omnibus of Sources,* edited by Marion A. Habig (Franciscan Herald Press, Chicago, 1973).

Our main objective in writing this book has been to examine certain deeper aspects of some of the most significant events in Francis's unique life, beginning with the cultural/spiritual setting into which he was born, leading ultimately to his writing of "The Canticle of the Creatures." This present book originated in a series of lectures given by Paul M. Allen held in connection with the observance of the eight-hundredth anniversary of the birth of Francis of Assisi. These lectures were given in Camphill Hall, Aberdeen; The Christian Community in Edinburgh; the Sheiling Community, Ringwood; Dunshane Camphill

Community, Republic of Ireland; Solborg and Vidaråsen Camphill Villages in Norway, and in other places as well.

This book has developed from the authors' many years of study and concern with the life and influence of Francis of Assisi, in the light of the concepts and ideas expressed by the Austrian philosopher and educator Rudolf Steiner (1861–1925) in his writings and lectures on anthroposophy, the modern science of spirit.

Paul M. and Joan deRis Allen
Corbenic Camphill Community
Perthshire, Scotland
Michaelmas, 1995

❧ 1 ☙

Francis of Assisi:
The Early Years

I f ever there has been a true Christian saint since the founding of Christianity, it was St. Francis. He has often been referred to as "everyone's favorite saint," designated as the patron saint of Italy, and in more recent years named the patron saint of ecology by Pope John Paul II in 1980. From his own time to ours, Francis of Assisi has been loved and appreciated in all parts of the world and among millions of people. This includes not only Christians but followers of many religions, a number of whom do not accept the Christian faith, nor the teachings of the Bible. The quality of love seemed to shine out from him in a way that no one could resist, and behind this genuine simplicity was a rare intuitive understanding of the life around him.

The life, work, and influence of Francis of Assisi can be understood in various ways. An immense literature about him exists in a number of languages and whole libraries have been established on this subject. Every little fact, every tradition, every detail of his life has been re-searched and discussed, and the work of an enormous number of schol-ars has accumulated during the more than eight hundred years since his birth. Therefore, the result of this great scholarship is one way by which Francis of Assisi can be understood. Nevertheless, despite its excellence, the fruits of this research have their limitations, and it may well be asked, Is there not another way to find access to Francis of Assisi?

Indeed there is. One can meet him in the remarkable number of recollections preserved about him. These wonderful little tales and unforgettable scenes, these heartwarming events and vignettes, have been included in that lovely volume, one of the most beautiful books in the religious literature of the world, *The Little Flowers of St. Francis* (*I Fioretti di San Francesco*). Truly it is a rare gem. Children love this book because of the unique glimpses it gives of the life and deeds of this gentle, unassuming man. Once these stories have been read, they cannot be easily forgotten, for in truth they are a rightful part of the heritage of every child. For adults as well, they continue to offer an intimate message beyond the details of scholarly research, however valuable the latter may be.

A third way one can come to know Francis of Assisi is through the work of the many artists inspired by the events of the forty-four years of his life. These artistic representations in the form of paintings, frescoes, drawings, sculptures, stained glass, and mosaics, give immediate visual access to many of the outstanding moments in the life of Saint Francis. In this connection one only need recall the twenty-eight magnificent frescoes by Giotto in the upper church of the basilica of Saint Francis in Assisi, a veritable biography of Francis's life in pictorial form. This is not to mention the outstanding paintings of Cimabue, Gozzoli, Fra Angelico, Berlingheri, Bellini, and many others, including artists of our own time.

A fourth, and perhaps the most living of the possible approaches to experiencing Francis, is to become aware of the unique relationship between the man and Assisi, the place of his birth and of the major scenes of his life. Above all, is this relationship not expressed in the fact that he is almost always referred to as Francis *of Assisi?* Truly, even today one can hardly think of Assisi without associating the place with the man, and one can scarcely imagine Francis himself separated from the physical surroundings that were so much a part of his entire life. In fact, among scholars who have spent a great part of their lives considering various aspects of Francis, there is a distinct question whether Francis made Assisi or whether Assisi made Francis.

However this may be, Assisi was already an important Etruscan town in the Umbrian landscape centuries before Francis was born. Later it was famous throughout the time of imperial Rome and the centuries that followed. For many people, even to this day, the three most important centers of Christian spirituality and pilgrimage are Jerusalem, Rome, and Assisi.

John Ruskin once wrote that Dante was "the central man of Florence." In a similar way it can be said that Francis, the *poverello*, the little poor man, was and remains "the central man of Assisi." Wherever

1. View of Assisi from the West. *(Photo by the authors.)*

one goes in Assisi these many centuries later, one still meets him at every turn, in every street, in the squares, in the daytime, in the nighttime. One experiences his living presence as a reality more than eight-hundred years later, as anyone well knows who has been fortunate enough to spend a longer time in Assisi. As Pope John XXIII once remarked: "Here, with Saint Francis, we are indeed at the gates of paradise. We may well ask, why did God give Assisi this enchantment of nature, this atmosphere of holiness as though suspended in the air, which the visitor experiences almost tangibly? So that men will come to recognize their creator and each other as brothers."

At his own request a few days before his death, Francis was carried from the bishop's palace in Assisi to the Porziuncola. A short distance from the town he asked his bearers to pause. Turning toward Assisi, blind as he was, he lifted his hands, and blessed the town with a prayer, concluding with the words: "May Assisi always remain the home of those who know and glorify God's blessed and glorious name throughout the ages to come."

As one approaches Assisi, crossing the Umbrian plain from the west, particularly at the hour of sunset, the town appears as a dreamlike mirage, resting on a spur of the western slopes of Mount Subasio. An almost magical grouping of houses, towers, churches, spires, walls, gateways—all of them made of local stone of a rosy-pink hue, and roofed with terracotta tiles in the local tradition—appear to draw together in a harmonious oneness in the light of the setting sun. At the northern extremity of the town, resting upon the steep rock cliffs, rise the mighty foundation walls supporting the many-storied cloister and the lower and upper churches of the basilica of Saint Francis. It was built less than a hundred years after his death in 1226. This enormous grouping of buildings is reminiscent of the dramatic gothic structure of Mont St. Michel in northern France. As this composition is viewed from the plain below, the observer is curiously reminded of another dramatic building massif, that of the Tibetan Potala Palace in Lhasa. It is as if at this moment the visitor to Assisi can experience something akin to an atmosphere of beneficent peace hovering over the town, a quality often associated with the Gautama Buddha.

Upon entering Assisi, passing through one of its ancient gateways in the gathering twilight—particularly at Michaelmas time when the autumnal mists arise from the plain below—one may ascend a narrow medieval street. The shuttered windows and silence create a mysterious atmosphere remarkable in its contrast to the colorful activity still taking place not far away in the brightly lighted squares of the town. Unexpectedly visitors may find themselves standing at the entrance to the *stalletta*, the little stable, where it is said that Francis, the son of Pietro and Pica Bernardone, was born at Michaelmas time, 1182.

Francis's father was one of the most important figures in the mercantile life of Assisi. His shop was filled with rich and costly fabrics, imported largely from France. Francis's mother was from Provence, and combined a deep sense of religious piety with a love for folktales, poetry, and music. While Francis's father was away on a business journey to France, the time for giving birth to their child was long overdue. His mother and the women of her household were in despair. It is said that at that moment a mysterious stranger appeared, knocked on the door, and told them that if the lady of the house were taken to the stable nearby and laid on the straw among the animals, she would very shortly give birth. This was immediately done and the child was born without further difficulty.

As visitors climb upward from the *stalletta*, cross the Piazza del Comune and continue along the Via San Rufino, they soon reach the square in front of the cathedral of San Rufino named for the patron saint of

Assisi. It was here that Francis was christened in 1182. Thirteen years later he was present at the baptism of an infant later to become well-known as Frederick II Hohenstaufen, who had been born in 1194 in the castle of Rocca Maggiore, dominating the heights above the town.

Francis eventually attended the school of San Giorgio, not far from his home, conducted by the canons of the cathedral of San Rufino. One of his lifelong memories from this time concerned the painting of the story about St. George and the dragon, pictured in a mural on one of the walls of the school. This tale was told to the students each year on April 23, St. George's day. Something of a dim stirring of admiration and desire to be a knight must have slowly arisen in him from this legend, and also from similar stories concerning knighthood told him by his mother.

Near the western end of the Piazza del Comune, the building still exists where Pietro Bernardone had his shop, in which he sold valuable fabrics including embroidered samite, soft velvets, damasks, and furs, as well as cloth of silver and gold threads. It was here that Francis began his apprenticeship in the family business at the age of fourteen. One day when he was at work, a beggar entered and asked for alms "in the name of Christ." Annoyed, Francis angrily sent him away emptyhanded. A short time later Francis was overcome by remorse for what he had done in response to the beggar's plea. He vowed to himself that if ever again anyone asked him for help in the name of Christ, he would never refuse to grant the request.

Like many of his friends, Francis having now nearly reached twenty years of age, was filled with fiery enthusiasm, idealism, and courage to become a knight and to join his comrades in the defense of Assisi. Accordingly, his parents gave him a fine horse and armor so that he was equipped to enter the army and take part in the war then taking place against the forces of Perugia. Across the plain, not far from Assisi, is Collestrada, the hill where the soldiers of Assisi suffered a severe defeat in November 1202. Many of the Assisians including Francis were captured at the time, and imprisoned under appalling conditions in Perugia. A little less than two years later, Francis was exchanged and allowed to return home, ill and a mere shadow of his former self. His recovery was slow and only after a considerable time was he able to rejoin his friends on another military expedition, this time toward the south. However his illness soon recurred and he was forced to remain in a monastery at Spoleto in order to regain his strength. One night he was awakened from sleep by a voice which spoke to him out of the darkness: "Who do you think can best reward you as a knight, the master or the servant?" Francis answered "The master." "Then why do you leave the master for the servant, the rich lord for the poor man?" Francis, convinced that this was the voice of the Christ, asked "Oh Lord, what do you want of me?" The voice replied "Return to Assisi and there you will learn what you are to do." Shortly afterwards, deeply moved by this experience, Francis once again found himself in his parents' house in Assisi, resuming the pattern of his former life.

Sometime after his return, the members of the Tripudianti—composed of a group of young men of wealth and position who devoted much of their time to social occasions, banqueting and entertaining beautiful young women in the style of the troubadours—held one of their festive gatherings. One can easily imagine walking along a quiet street in Assisi at night, when suddenly the sound of instrumental music accompanying youthful singing is heard. Glimpses of flaming torches carried by flower-garlanded figures are seen. These are the members of the Tripudianti, riotously dancing their way along the street, led by the head of the merrymakers, none other than Francis himself! Yet, despite all this carefree revelry, it was on this very night that Francis was to discover why he had been directed to return to Assisi, where he would learn what his life task was to be. On this fateful evening, beneath the star-filled heavens, Francis for the first time came face-to-face with the mysterious, hitherto unknown one, who later was to become the lady of his heart, the inspirer and guardian of his future knighthood. She would become his "bride," to her service he would pledge himself without reserve, remaining faithful to her to his last breath. Her name was Poverty. Of her he was later to write: "Poverty is to have nothing, to wish for nothing, yet to possess all things truly in the spirit of freedom."

After this meeting, Francis's life was never to be the same again. Following this silent, mysterious event, a time of restless searching led him day after day from one place to another in the wonderful countryside around Assisi. Meditation and prayer became his daily food, his nourishment, as he walked over the verdant hills, stopping in the peaceful quiet of small churches, abandoned chapels, and kneeling before wayside shrines. For him, all these became places of intense spiritual devotion and contemplation. At last, the crucial moment arrived when his steps led him to visit the small, half-ruined church of San Damiano, not far outside the walls of Assisi itself. More or less abandoned, it had long before fallen into disuse. An old priest who lived nearby infrequently celebrated Mass there, keeping the place open, but was able to do very little to maintain it in good repair.

Today as one walks along the pathway leading from Assisi to the ancient church of San Damiano, one is surrounded by solemn dark green cedars and brightly shimmering silver-leafed olive trees. Here one can easily imagine the day when Francis followed this same road and at length found himself in the dimness of the long, narrow nave of the church, its thick, crumbling walls green with age. As he knelt, praying and mediating hour after hour, he often lifted his eyes to the Byzantine crucifix hanging high above in front of the altar. Then it was that he had one of the greatest spiritual experiences of his entire life. He heard the crucifix speaking words to him he would never forget: "Go Francis, and repair my church, which as you see, is falling into ruin." These words perhaps could be better rendered as: "Go Francis, and repair my church, which as you see, is being destroyed." This was a tremendous moment and made an overwhelming impact upon Francis, for to him it was a kind of Michaelic call. Now at long last he knew clearly what his task was to be. On his wanderings he had observed that in Assisi, and particularly in the surrounding countryside, were many little churches and chapels, most of them extremely old. With the passage of time, they were sorely in need of repair or rebuilding.

At once Francis responded to the voice from the crucifix, and began the work of restoring San Damiano with his own hands. However, at this point one could possibly ask; who was doing the destroying, and where was the "church" spoken of by the voice from the crucifix? One could regard the church or house as existing within Francis himself. In other words, it was he, Francis, who was destroying this house, his inner house. It was the course of his own life that was in need of change, of transformation, although possibly Francis did not fully grasp this at first.

However, Francis soon realized that money would be needed in order to obtain the materials necessary to restore these buildings. Fired by determined purpose, and without a second thought, he took a roll of most valuable embroidery from his father's shop and without difficulty he exchanged it for gold in the marketplace at Foligno. Overjoyed, he returned to San Damiano and showing the gold to the old priest, he

2. The crucifix that spoke to Francis in San Damiano. Now preserved in the Basilica of Sta. Chiara, Assisi.

exclaimed: "Now I can buy what I need to repair this church!" Terrified of Pietro Bernardone's well-known anger, the old man tried to persuade Francis to give the gold to his father, but the young man emphatically refused to do so. Consequently, it was not long before Francis was summoned to appear before Bishop Guido to account for his actions.

Today, under the stone archway on the south side of the Piazza del Comune, there is a long, winding series of stone steps, passing near the *stalleta*. From there the way continues steeply downward to the quiet, tree-lined Piazza Vescovada. On the left side of the square, stands the venerable Romanesque church of Santa Maria Maggiore, the original cathedral of Assisi. Straight ahead at the end of the street, stand the gates leading into the forecourt of the Vescovado, the residence of the bishop of Assisi.

This spot is familiar to many from the paintings of Giotto and Gozzoli, both of whom depicted the dramatic event that occurred here in 1207. As one recalls these frescoes—one of them in the upper basilica of San Francesco in Assisi, the other in the ancient Franciscan church in Montefalco—the entire fateful moment comes to life once again. The courtyard is crowded with men of every rank and social position, young and old alike. They have come to attend this session of the bishop's court, called in response to a complaint made by the wealthy merchant Pietro Bernardone, demanding that his son Francis be punished for having stolen and sold valuable goods from his shop. The outraged father demands justice from Bishop Guido. However, before the latter can reply, Francis suddenly strips off his clothing and places it with the gold he had received in payment for the goods, at his father's feet saying, "Until this day I have called Pietro Bernardone my father, but from now on I can say, without reserve, "Our Father, who art in Heaven."

A profound startled silence follows these words. Bishop Guido stands as though transfixed. Although he was a servant of the church, he was nevertheless a man of quick temper, an ardent defender of property rights, himself the owner of many castles, much land, and a multitude of serfs. Clearly, he now finds himself in an extraordinary dilemma: should he defend the rights of a fellow property owner, or should he listen to the unexpected promptings of his own heart and conscience? Almost without thinking, he draws the young man to his side and silently wraps his bishop's cloak around Francis's body. The gesture is eloquent beyond words, the implication is clear: through this action

3. Francis and his father before Bishop Guido. Fresco by Benozzo Gozzoli (1421–1497), Montefalco. *(Postcard published by Electa, Italy–A0364.)*

of Bishop Guido, Francis was taken under the care and protection of the church from that moment onward.

A long, half-audible sigh follows, as the onlookers, most of them having gathered with the hope of seeing a drama of severe punishment meted out, slowly turn away, puzzled and somehow disappointed. As the bishop silently and resolutely mounts the stairs leading into his residence, Pietro Bernardone, in cold rage and filled with the bitterness of defeat in the presence of so many of his fellow citizens, gathers up the clothes and the gold, and pushes his way through the silent throng.

Meanwhile, as though following the words of Saint Jerome spoken long ago: (*nudam crucem nudus sequar*) "Naked, I follow the naked cross," Francis wandered into the bishop's orchard. One of the kindly gardeners gave him a worker's castoff, ragged garment to wear. This rough cloak was made of *tintinello*, a material loosely woven of cotton and very little wool, commonly used for the clothing of lepers. Later, finding a piece of chalk, Francis drew a large cross on the back of it.

Alone, Francis left Assisi behind him with firm, sure steps as the night was coming on, wandering northward through the lonely mountains in the direction of Gubbio. However, judging by the shining expression in his face, depicted in both frescoes mentioned above, in the deeper sense he was by no means *alone*. An early biographer, who well may have spoken to people who had been present on the occasion, reported that as Francis stood before the bishop, one of his hands appeared to be holding the hand of another person standing beside him, invisible to everyone present. Was this the hand of his chosen bride? Was this the moment of his wedding? In this moment, had he married Poverty, in whose service from then onward, at whatever cost, he was to remain faithful to the end of his life?

❧ 2 ☙

The Spiritual-Historical
Background of Francis of Assisi

In order to grasp the extraordinary significance of Saint Francis, it is essential first of all to take into account something of the political, social, and religious influences at work during his lifetime, not only in Assisi but in Italy and far beyond its borders. Without doubt, it is not a matter of mere chance where a person is born and where the events of one's life occur. This is particularly true in relation to Francis and the role he was ultimately destined to play in the unfolding historical scene in Italy and in the wider world, both during and after his lifetime.

The outstanding political character of the historical setting into which Francis was born was one of constant conflict expressed in an uncompromising struggle and rivalry between the temporal aims and aspirations of the feudal lords, knights, and landowners. This culminated in the figure of the Holy Roman Emperor on the one hand, and on the other hand, the ever-widening extent of papal ambition, exemplified in the personality and activity of Innocent III and the church at large. Amid these bitter confrontations, there gradually arose a third factor in the form of a newly emerging merchant class. Indeed, it was precisely this threefold struggle that characterized the political life in twelfth-century Italy. As a son of one of the most prominent members of the mercantile class in Assisi, Francis had ample opportunity to experience and share the effects of this conflict at first hand, for example in the defeat of the army of Assisi in the battle of Collestrada, and in his own capture and imprisonment in Perugia.

The social conditions in Assisi as well as in many other Italian towns at that time were appalling due to this constant political strife. The brutal effects of the class system manifested themselves in an implacable serfdom suffered by a large share of the population, as well as the utterly inhumane treatment and nearly universal rejection of lepers, cripples, the insane, the aged, the poverty-stricken, and handicapped persons everywhere. In sharp contrast to the underprivileged multitudes forming by far the largest social group in the country, stood the small minority composed of the ruling upper classes. These wealthy, noble families, feudal warlords and embattled knights, possessed virtually absolute power of life and death over the others. Often their unscrupulous lust for power, privilege, and possessions, the licentiousness of their personal lifestyle, as well as their frequently heartless treatment of their fellow human beings, were all too often characteristic of the social life in Assisi when Francis was a youth.

Despite all these circumstances in political and social life, certain aspects of the religious life of the time amply justify the fact that these centuries are often referred to as the Age of Faith. Nevertheless, when the history of the twelfth century is penetrated, disturbing contradictions are confronted, even in the religious life as it then manifested itself. Many ancient, venerated churches and chapels, particularly in the countryside around places like Assisi, were sadly neglected and partially destroyed. Among the higher clergy especially, striving after personal gain and political influence was rampant. Many fighting bishops, monks, and other clergymen frequently wore armor under their habits, thus bearing arms in violation of Christ's teaching of universal peace. Added to this, under the leadership and ardent instigation of Innocent III, a time of terrible persecution and destruction of many minority groups took place, who were regarded as heretics. They included the Albigensians, the Cathars, the Waldensians, the poor little men of Lyons, and later, even the order of the Knights Templar.

It was against the background of this political, social, and religious life that the miracle of Francis of Assisi unfolded. Into the confusion, cruelty, and darkness of this time, Francis was able to bring *pace et bene*, peace and goodness, to his surroundings. He fulfilled to the utmost in the course of his life the words of his own prayer:

> Lord, make me an instrument of your peace,
> Where there is hatred, let me sow love.
> Where there is injury, let me sow pardon.
> Where there is discord, let me sow unity.

Where there is doubt, let me sow faith.
Where there is despair, let me sow hope.
Where there is sadness, let me sow joy.
Where there is darkness, let me sow light.
O Divine Master, grant that I may not so much seek
To be consoled, as to console.
To be understood, as to understand.
To be loved, as to love.
For it is in giving, that we receive.
It is in pardoning, that we are pardoned.
It is in dying, that we are born into eternal life.

*   *   *

The life of Francis becomes even more historically and spiritually significant when one views it against the succession of events taking place in the wider world beyond Assisi between 1152 (thirty years prior to his birth) and 1228 (the year of his canonization):

1152	Frederick 1 Hohenstaufen becomes King
1167	Frederick 1 Hohenstaufen crowned as Holy Roman Emperor
1167	Oxford University founded
1170	Thomas à Becket murdered in Canterbury Cathedral
1163– 1235	Notre Dame Cathedral constructed in Paris
1172	Wolfram von Eschenbach and Walther von der Vogelweide born
1178	Snorri Sturlason born in Iceland (wrote the Heimskringla Saga of the Norwegian Kings)
1182	Birth of Francis of Assisi
1185	Branch of the Knights Templar established in London (original order founded in Jerusalem, 1118)
1187	Saladin recaptures Jerusalem
1189	Richard I, Coeur-de-Lion, became king of England
1193	Albertus Magnus born (died 1280)
1194	Chartres Cathedral begun (consecrated 1260)
1195	Anthony of Padova born (died 1231)
1198	Innocent III became pope, reigning to 1216 (This was also a time of almost continual strife between kings, higher clergy, and feudal lords.)

1203	*Parzival* written by Wolfram von Eschenbach
1204	Crusaders capture Constantinople
1207	Saint Elizabeth of Hungary born
1209	Francis of Assisi issues first Rule
1214	Roger Bacon, English scientist, born
1215	Dominican Order founded
1215	Magna Carta
1220	Dominican Rule confirmed by Pope Honorius III
1220	Frederick II crowned Holy Roman Emperor in Rome
1223	Franciscan Rule confirmed by Pope Honorius III
1225	Thomas Aquinas born (died 1274)
1226	Francis of Assisi died
1227	Gregory IX became Pope (to 1241)
1228	Pope Gregory IX canonized Francis of Assisi

In addition, this was also the age of many of the great Christian mystics (1200–1400), including Johannes Tauler, Meister Eckhart, and Heinrich Suso. Anyone who considers the turbulent conflicting currents of the Middle Ages described above, can find them reflected in these moving lines written by the famous minnesinger poet, Walther von der Vogelweide (1172–c. 1230):

I fell to wondering
Why man was on earth at all.
No answer came to me;
How men may come by these three things,
So that no man need perish:
Two of these are Honor and Worldly Goods;
These often do each other harm.
The third, the most important,
Is that men *Please God.*
Yet I long to have all three of them
Enclosed within a single shrine.
But, Alas, that can never be!
For Worldly Goods and Honor
Together with the grace of God,
Dwell not within a single human heart.
Hindrances are present everywhere,

Faithlessness sets endless snares,
Brute force lays all men low.
Peace and Right are done to death.
Never will the Three find place together
Till these first two are fully healed and well-restored.

•   •   •

When Rudolf Steiner took up his residence in Berlin in 1899 at the conclusion of his work as an editor of Goethe's natural scientific writings, included in the collected edition of the latter's work, published under the auspices of the Goethe/Schiller Archive in Weimar, he was visited by a committee inviting him to join the faculty of an adult education college for working people. Asked if he would be willing to speak about history, he replied: "I would be happy to give such a course, but the question is whether you would like to hear about *my* kind of history."

One might ask what he implied in his expression "my kind of history." Perhaps an indication of this can be found in the title of two lectures given by him at Dornach, Switzerland, on March 16 and 17, 1923: "Human History as a Reflection of Supersensible Events Working Through Spiritual Powers" and "The Battle between Progressive and Retarding Hierarchical Beings from the Fourth Century Onwards."

It is indeed extraordinary to imagine *battles* taking place in the spiritual world. The thought of earthly history as a reflection of supersensible events, including strife between hierarchical beings, may at first be startling, until the words at the opening of the famous twelfth chapter of the Book of Revelation by Saint John are recalled: "And there was war in heaven. . . ." This is truly an arresting statement: the idea of war taking place in heaven is not customary; heaven is rather imagined as an entirely quiet, harmonious, peaceful place. However, heaven is not a place at all, but as Christ himself said: "The kingdom of heaven is within you." Heaven is in no sense of the word a *place*, but is a setting for the activity of spiritual beings. Moreover, heaven is entirely nonspatial, nontemporal; it is solely a state of being in the nature of infinity.

At about the time when Francis of Assisi lived, one of the frequent subjects of discussion among theologians was the question: "How many angels can stand upon the point of a pin at any one time?" This is by no means an empty query. It can be answered in two ways: either no angels or an infinite number of angels can stand upon the point of a pin at any one time, depending upon one's concept of existing spatial and temporal relationships. For the beings of the spiritual world are concerned with neither space nor time.

A similar theme appears in *The Divine Comedy*, by Dante Alighieri (1265–1321), written less than a hundred years after the death of Francis of Assisi. The atmosphere of *The Paradiso*, forming the third part of this mighty work, is permeated by four qualities: light, sound, motion, and joy. Of these, light is unmistakably the first in importance, infinite, and the most all-pervading, as the opening lines of the first Canto show:

> La glória di colui che tutto move
> Per l'universo penetra, e risplende
> In una parte più, e meno altrove.

> The light of Him who moveth everything
> Doth penetrate the universe, and shine
> In one part more and in another less.

In the fifth Canto this is developed further in the words:

> Del lume che per tutto il ciel si spazia
> Noi semo accesi: e però, se disii
> Da noi chiarirti, a tuo piacer ti sazia.

> With light that through the whole of heaven is outspread
> Kindled are we, and hence if thou desirest
> To know of us, at thine own pleasure, sate thee.
> —*Longfellow, trans.*

This concept of light-filled infinity is not easy to grasp. The moment heaven is thought of, one must think of a condition existing outside our understanding of the limits of space and time. Here one can note that the word *infinite* involves a comparatively modern idea, first developed by Cardinal Nicholas of Cusa (1401–1464). Rudolf Steiner discusses Cusa at length in his book *Mysticism at the Dawn of the Modern Age* (see the Introduction to the 1960 English translation, pages 50–54). Therefore, it becomes clear that in order to grasp the true nature of heaven, or the spiritual world, one is faced with the almost impossible necessity of thinking beyond the limits of space and time.

In sharp contrast to this, Mark Twain, in his delightfully humorous book *Captain Stormfield's Trip to Heaven*, parodies those concepts, those limited, dogmatic attitudes so characteristic of the materialism dominating much religious thinking in the latter part of nineteenth-century America.

When Captain Stormfield arrives at the gates of heaven, he is provided with a pair of wings, a halo, a palm branch, a harp, and a hymn book. He is assigned a place where he can sit on a cloud together with a multitude of the elect. However, it is not long before heaven becomes boring for him, considering that he never had much taste for music or harp-playing, and above all he totally lacked any experience in flying. In addition, sitting on a damp cloud, waving a palm branch all day, soon became rather tedious, and the mere thought of doing this for all eternity absolutely dismayed him. Finally the moment comes when in desperation he turns to one of his companions, inquiring: "How long do I have to go on doing this?" The latter laughingly replies: "That's what we've been waiting for you to ask!" Without delay, the captain throws away the wings and halo, sets aside the palm branch and hymn book, lays down the harp, gratefully arises from the damp cloud, and is escorted to more enjoyable and interesting regions of heaven.

In the opening sentence of his doctoral thesis (1892) Rudolf Steiner pointed out that "our age suffers from an unhealthy faith in Kant." It is clear that the boundaries of knowledge set up by Kant have their fruit in that materialistic view characterized in Mark Twain's delightful story of life in the heavenly world. Certain traces of Kant's point of view unfortunately remain alive within many people even today. Because of this, one can at first be startled when confronted by a picture of the spiritual world that involves the working of spiritual beings, both positive and negative.

However, if one thinks of the spiritual world, of heaven, as *a condition of widened consciousness*, broadened far beyond the scope of our ordinary intellectual thinking, one can better glimpse what was implied in Rudolf Steiner's expression "my kind of history." How is it possible to understand the world of Francis of Assisi in the light of what Rudolf Steiner in our time has described as "Human History as a Reflection of Supersensible Events Occurring from the Fourth Century Onward"? The first requirement is to learn how to widen our consciousness, how to take the initial step toward breaking down those barriers, those boundaries of knowledge that Immanuel Kant (1724–1804) erected in his philosophy. To remedy this, one can begin to strive toward what Samuel Longfellow described as "the freer step, the fuller breath, the wide horizon's grander view." This process is clearly outlined in Rudolf Steiner's book *How Can One Attain Knowledge of Higher Worlds?*, which opens with the challenging sentence: "There slumber within *every* human being faculties by means of which he can, for himself, attain knowledge of higher worlds."

*   *   *

From old traditions, many of them based upon the spiritual investigations of the renowned Benedictine scholar and historian Johannes Trithemius, Abbot of Sponheim (1462–1560), human history can be divided into distinct periods of approximately three hundred fifty years each. Trithemius taught that each of these periods in turn functions under the influence of a particular archangel. In line with this teaching, history is said to be governed by a series of seven leading archangels, among whom are Raphael (God heals), Gabriel (the messenger of God), Uriel (the fire of God), and in our time, since 1879, Michael (who is like God?). In this light, the forty-four years of Francis of Assisi's life (1182–1226) fall during the period when the Archangel Samael influenced the guidance of human affairs.

Since the guiding archangel in Francis's lifetime was Samael, whose name means "God asks," the question naturally arises; "What did God ask in that moment of history?" To Francis and his companions, there was but one answer: "God asks that we serve him." Indeed men like Francis strove to serve God in every conceivable way. Thus arose the Age of Faith, characterized by pilgrimages of the devout, the time of the crusades, the cathedral builders, the school of Chartres, the era of the great Scholastics: Thomas Aquinas, Albertus Magnus, Saint Dominic, and a number of others. The lives and achievements of these individuals, as well as the conditions under which they lived and worked, can be regarded as the earthly manifestations of the divine demand that God was placing before humanity at that particular time. At this point it is helpful to consider the words of Rudolf Steiner from his lecture of March 17, 1923, mentioned above:

"Everything that happens between the fourth and the twelfth century (that is roughly between the 300s and the 1100s, the time during which Francis lived), everything that happens between the fourth and twelfth centuries is a reflection of the battle between certain beings of the spiritual world, between the Archai, Spirits of Personality, and the retarded Exusiai, Spirits of Form, regarding the world of thought." (See chapter 7, *The World of the Celestial Hierarchies.*)

In order to understand something of the spiritual events referred to in this statement, it is first of all necessary to imagine Europe as it was during the Middle Ages. If one regards Assisi as the center point in relation to the four cardinal directions, one can recognize that out of Scandinavia in the north, a powerful movement extends itself under the guidance of archangelic beings, whose influence has been described as that of a "white fire," a kind of "white magic." These progressive, beneficent archangels guided the Norsemen in their search for what traditionally came to be known as Mikaelgård, Michael's home, the "home" of the Archangel Michael. The elemental power of this impulse arising out of the north is expressed to a certain extent in the themes of the Icelandic eddas as well as in Norse myths and sagas. This migration subsequently took its course in two directions. One of these was led by the Vikings toward the west and south, following the northern coast of Scotland to the Hebrides and Ireland, thence into what is now northern France, along the coast of Spain, and even to Italy itself. At approximately the same time, a second wave of Norsemen moved eastward into the Slavic lands, following the course of the great rivers of the central Russian plain, on their way establishing centers from which they could then move still further to the south, eventually to the area of the Black Sea and Constantinople.

This twofold quest, this longing to discover what in Christian terms they called the "home" of the Archangel Michael, their desire to reach this new and fabled place, led them westward and eastward out of the north, thus forming a great encircling movement, enclosing the heart of Europe.

Steiner also indicated that from the west, a very different hierarchical influence emerged, inspired by the Archai, the spirits of personality, those beings who guide the successive historical epochs of time. The Archai are the bearers of what is particularly individual in each human being, that precious, unique element that is his or her essential nature. This "I" forms the basis of each person's uniqueness and gives the possibility for his or her freedom. Guided by this spiritual, hierarchical impulse, the Celtic peoples gradually moved from the west into the heart of Europe.

In the east a quite different influence arose ultimately changing the entire character of the Middle Ages. From this direction came the activity of the "retarding Exusiai," spirits of form. These spiritual beings strove to upset the normal balance exerted by the Archai described above, whose objective was to allow the "I" of man to shine forth. Thus it became exceedingly difficult for the individual "I" to manifest itself freely in the disordered world of the east, where the decadent, tormented influences arising out of central Asia, fostering the "herd instinct," slowly pressed westward into Europe. Moreover, this movement broke into two streams, the one working out of the northeast, forming the Mongol and Hunic invasions, the other driving the Turks in a southwesterly direction into what is now Greece, the Balkans, and northern Italy.

The fourth spiritual stream acting behind the outer historical events of these centuries, as Steiner describes, came from the south, appearing in the region of North Africa. This activity was entirely different in character from that of the archangelic beings of the Scandinavian north, who had inspired the development of history in a positive way. Now from the south came the impulses of the "hindering archangels" who worked in opposition to the constructive influences coming from the north.

Two spiritual centers now arose as a result of these basically contrasting movements: in the north of France the Platonist-inspired mystical School of Chartres, in the south the Aristotelian-inspired scientific school in Sicily. However, the impulses of these two differing schools eventually were brought into a state of balance, due to the appearance of a third spiritual influence—namely, that of the Holy Grail, sometimes referred to as the Ganganda Greida, the Wandering Grail, the Viaticum. Out of this impulse moving across southern Europe arose centers of the Grail tradition in what is now Provence, northern Spain, and Portugal. These Grail centers formed the source of the inspiration motivating Chrétien de Troye's (1144–1190) Grail stories and later that of Wolfram Von Eschenbach's Parzival epic, which appeared in 1203, when Francis was twenty-one.

A second manifestation of the working of the Grail impulse, particularly during the time of Francis of Assisi, was the marked change of consciousness reflected in the artistic representations of the virgin in painting, sculpture, stained glass, and mosaics. These changes stand in strong contrast to the somewhat remote, even stern expression of the virgin as hitherto portrayed in Byzantine and Romanesque art. Now something of the tender heart forces that were to characterize Francis himself appeared in the gentle, slightly smiling countenance and comforting, enfolding gestures of the youthful virgin. This new style of representation opened the way for what ultimately was to attain consummate perfection in the madonnas of Raphael some two hundred years later. Clearly this remarkable change can be viewed as an expression of something of the loving attitude, the striving for "peace and goodness" that formed the example, teaching, and life of Francis of Assisi.

Thus one can see that the appearance of these Grail centers brought a number of remarkable humanizing, beneficial results during this period of history. These centers of the Grail mysteries gradually exerted a balancing effect, particularly between the school in Sicily, led by its great Islamic scholars, teachers of medicine, philosophy, astronomy, and mathematics, coming across the Mediterranean from North Africa to southern Spain, Sicily, and Italy on the one hand, and the School of Chartres on the other, inspired by the Celtic Christian world of nature-mysticism, arising in part from the activities of the Normans and Vikings, and in part through the influences of the ancient Druids.

Another particularly important activity of these times was centered in Rome. It was here that the worldly power and temporal influence of the papacy reached a higher point than ever before or since, under the guidance and domination of Pope Innocent III, during whose papacy the administrative strength and wealth of the church were enormous. It was to Innocent III that Francis and his twelve companions turned to request recognition of the First Rule of his Order, and it was this pope who gave them the name of Friars Minor (*Fratri Minori*).

In a lecture given by Rudolf Steiner, "The History of the Middle Ages" (Berlin, 1904), he described the marked contrast between the politically orientated members of the high ranking clergy and the members of the monastic orders:

> Princes, dukes, kings, even poets, unless they were ecclesiastics, could seldom read or write. Wolfram von Eschenbach had to dictate his poems to a clergyman and let him read them aloud to him; and Hartmann von Aue boasts as a special accomplishment, that he

can read books. In all secular culture at that time there was no question of reading and writing. Only in the enclosed monasteries were Art and Science studied. All other students were directed to what was offered them in the teaching and preaching of the clergy, and that brought about the dependence on the clergy and the monks; it gave the church its indisputable authority. The latter was enhanced by the fact that it was the clergy themselves who carried out all the arrangements for promoting knowledge. The monks were the church architects, it was they who adorned the buildings with statues, they who copied the works of classical authors in artistic, illuminated manuscripts. The higher officials, too, the emperor's chancellors, were, for the most part, monks. Even the mighty emperor Charlemagne in his old age finally undertook to learn to read and write. A great difference existed between the secularized clergy and those in the monasteries. The lower clergy governed by the bishops were mostly uneducated, unable to read and write, and of boorish manners. The bishops busied themselves with the administration of their property, they made profit out of their feudal tenants, and were as uneducated as the knights or peasants. Nothing of what we may call culture existed. This situation made it possible to consolidate and govern the church ever more and more, from Rome, as its center. However, it was different in the monasteries, where remarkable learning was to be found. All the education of these days proceeded entirely from the monasteries. In this manner they did not allow themselves to be made dependent on the political power of Rome, which was based on the secular ascendancy of the clergy.

Yet another spiritual-historical movement arose during the Middle Ages. This was inspired by the Normans and was led by prominent rulers from Scotland, England, France, Austria, who together with a great multitude of followers streamed toward the Middle East in order to rescue the Holy Places of Christianity from Islamic domination. It was the church which instigated, inspired, and directed these waves of military activity of the crusades, involving the lives and destinies of millions of human beings.

Tragically, when the crusaders reached the shores of Asia Minor, they began to loose all traces of their individual humanity and idealism, which as Rudolf Steiner indicated, the Archai, the spirits of personality, from the West had inspired in them. For the most part they forfeited their awareness of the individual "I" and were swept up before the onrush of the implacable "herd instinct" of the Islamic Middle East. Their Christian faith and motivation gave way to bestial licentiousness, unbridled cruelty, greed, lust, and lechery on a scale difficult to imagine at this distance.

All of this was observed first hand by Francis of Assisi himself, in witnessing the tragic events surrounding the siege of Damietta at the mouth of the Nile, and its terrible consequences, when a city of eighty-five thousand inhabitants was reduced to about three thousand, thus becoming a veritable "city of the dead."

The inevitable result of the devastating events arising from the crusades reached a climax around the year 1250, when as Rudolf Steiner describes in his book *The Spiritual Guidance of Man and Humanity*, a general darkening of human consciousness set in, so far as the individual's capacity of direct vision and experience of the reality of the spiritual world was concerned. This phenomenon marks a radical change of consciousness, slowly leading to the dawn of our modern age, heralded by the Renaissance, in the fifteenth century.

*   *   *

Into this setting which was shaped by hidden spiritual-cultural influences described above, resulting from the turbulent "struggles between progressive and retarding hierarchical beings" working behind outer historical events from the fourth century onwards, the individuality of Francesco Bernardone incarnated in Assisi in 1182.

In Francis' life, the search for "Michael's home," originating as we have seen among the peoples of the Scandinavian lands, found a unique expression. He was indeed a truly Michaelic spirit, a fact made evident in that many of the significant events of his forty-four years of life and the working of his destiny bore an unmistakable stamp of the guidance of the Archangel Michael. His earthly life began at Michaelmas time 1182, was fulfilled by his receiving the stigmata at Michaelmas 1224, and was finally consummated by his death shortly after Michaelmas, two years later on October 3, 1226. It is therefore entirely clear that Francis of Assisi was profoundly inspired and guided by the influence of the Archangel Michael throughout his entire life.

To return to the historical period in which Francis lived, this was led, according to the reckoning of Trithemius of Sponheim, by the

Archangel Samael, whose name means "God asks." And in the time of Francis, what did God ask? The answer is to be found in the entire life and striving of Francis of Assisi, who knew beyond all shadow of doubt that God asks that humans serve him. His total unreserved faithfulness in serving God and his complete devotion to his Lady Poverty is fully expressed in Francis's own words quoted above: "Poverty is to have nothing, to wish for nothing, yet to possess everything truly in the spirit of freedom."

❦ 3 ❦

The Knighthood of Compassion:
Francis's Damascus Experience

This is how God inspired me, Brother Francis, to embark upon a life of penance. When I was in sin, the sight of lepers nauseated me beyond measure; but then God himself led me into their company, and I had pity on them. When I had once become acquainted with them, what had previously nauseated me became a source of spiritual and physical consolation for me.

These profoundly moving words, written only a few days before his death on October 3, 1226, stand at the beginning of the last testament of St. Francis. They bear unmistakable confirmation of the Michaelic spirit, humanity, and courage that motivated the man in his entire earthly life and work. They bear witness to a clear recognition that it was the lepers and their terrible fate that stirred his being to its very depths, moving his heart and guiding his will along paths that markedly contributed to forming him into the saintly human being he ultimately became.

Recognizing this, Rudolf Steiner said:

Francis of Assisi was surrounded by people afflicted with very serious diseases such as leprosy, for which the world at that time knew no cure. Moral impulses were so powerful in him that many lepers through him were given spiritual aid and great comfort. It is true that many could gain no more—but there were many others who by their faith and trust attained a stage where the moral impulses and forces which poured forth from Francis of Assisi had a healing, health-giving effect. [Lecture given at Norköping, Sweden, May 29, 1912]

* * *

One of the darkest chapters in the long history of humankind's inhumanity concerns the terrible treatment of lepers in the Middle Ages, particularly in Italy. Leprosy had long been known in western Europe and seems to have been exacerbated by the terror and fear among the peoples of middle Europe as a result of the Hunnish and Mongol invasions from the east. In addition, during the crusades, in the time of Francis, an especially virulent form of this disease became rampant in many countries, from Italy in the south to the Scandinavian lands in the north. It is understandable that the physical symptoms resulting from this disease caused extreme fear and loathing everywhere. The typical lepers were pale specters, with blood-stained faces, shaved heads, their bodies dressed in gray sackcloth. Their emaciated, white faces often had pus dripping from open sores, and hideous eyes fearfully peering about them.

Although it is generally known that Francis and his companions undertook as a central task of their lives to minister and care for the lepers whom they often referred to as "the true Christians," it is difficult in our time to form a clear idea of the terrible scourge of leprosy in the medieval world, and its devastating effects upon the lives and destinies of its victims. Consequently it is not easy to grasp how it was that Francis attained the compassion for the lepers that he described in his last testament, without an understanding of the tragic lives of these people in his time.

Arnaldo Fortini, a prominent figure in the political and social life of Assisi earlier in our century, as well as a noted writer and authority on the life of St. Francis, found in his researches in the archives at Assisi original materials concerning the service for the reception of lepers into hospitals in the Middle Ages. Without doubt this service was the one customarily used in the leper hospital of San Lazzaro near Assisi. The following is a rendition of the substance of a part of Fortini's reconstruction of this material given in his monumental biography *Francis of Assisi,* translated by Helen Moak, Crossroad Publishing Co., New York, 1981. (*Nova Vita di San Francesco,* Tipografia Porziuncola, Santa Maria degli Angeli, 1959, 5 vols.).

4. Francis ministering to a leper. Drawing by E. Burnand. (From P. Vittirio Facchinetti, O.F.M., *San Francesco d'Assisi, nella storia, nella leggenda, nell'arte.* Milan: Casa Editrice, S. Lega Eucaristica, 1921, p. 347.)

In Francis's time, people hid the fact that they were lepers for as long as possible, until someone finally betrayed them and their illness became generally known. These afflicted ones, regardless whether man, woman, or child, were at once forcibly dragged from their homes, families, and friends, taken to such a leper hospital as San Lazzaro near Assisi, and confined there until the moment came when they were to be finally separated from their fellow humans for the remainder of their lives.

The leper was brought into the hospital chapel and forced to kneel before the altar. At that moment, as one can well imagine, his heart is filled with fear, hatred, and despair. The bell rings, the priest appears with his acolytes, and sprinkling holy water on the pathetic figure kneeling there, with the same gesture as is used for one who has died, he addresses him or her with this admonition:

> My brother, dear poor little man of the good God, by means of great sadness and tribulation, of sickness, of leprosy, and of many other miseries, one gains the kingdom of heaven, where there is

no sickness or sorrow, and all is pure and white, without stain, more brilliant than the sun. You will go there, if it pleases God. In the meantime, be a good Christian, bear with patience this adversity, and God will be merciful to you.

These words fall into a profound silence. The living corpse bends still closer to the ground and seems as though searching for its grave. The priest continues:

My brother, this separation has to do only with your body. As for the spirit, which is more important, you are still, as you were before, a participant in the prayers of our holy mother church, as if every day you were assisting in the divine office. Charitable men will provide for your lesser needs, and God will never abandon you. Take care of yourself and have patience. God is with you. Amen.

From the hands of an acolyte the priest then takes a handful of black earth brought from the cemetery nearby and sprinkles it over the head and body of the one kneeling before him. The prayer continues:

Die to the world, be born again in God. O Jesus my Redeemer, who made me of earth and clothed me with a body, make me to rise again in the new day.

(These words in the ritual reflect something of the spirit of the classical Rosicrucian formulation as given in seventeenth-century sources, often referred to by Rudolf Steiner and others: *ex Deo nascimur* (out of the divine, mankind takes being), *in Christo Morimur* (in Christ, death becomes life), *per Spiritum Sanctum reviviscimus* (through the Holy Spirit we are reborn). The similarity between this and Fortini's rendition quoted above is both striking and significant.)

The people respond, "My bones tremble, my soul loses its way. Alleluia. Have mercy on us, O Lord. Keep us from evil." As the congregation stands, the Gospel story from St. Luke about the healing of the ten lepers is read. The moment has now come for the instructions, which will inexorably separate him or her from the rest of humankind:

My brother, take this cloak and put it on as a sign of humility and never leave here without it. In the name of the Father, the Son, and the Holy Spirit.

The tunic, made of *tintinello*, the cheapest and roughest of material, reaches completely to the ground. Slowly, reluctantly, the leper puts it on. It is the ominous garment that will make people flee from the lepers wherever they go:

> Take this little flask. Put in it what will be given you to drink, and under penalty of disobedience I forbid you to drink from the rivers, the springs, the wells, wherever you go. Take these gloves. You are forbidden to touch anything that is not yours with your bare hands. If, while walking about, you should meet someone who wishes to talk to you, I forbid you to reply before you put yourself against the wind. You are forbidden to be with any woman who is not of your family. You are forbidden to touch young people or to offer them anything. You are forbidden to eat from anything but your own leper's bowl. You are forbidden to enter churches or rectories, and from going to fairs, to mills or markets. You are forbidden to walk through narrow streets where these who meet you cannot avoid you.

Finally, the leper is given the wooden clapper, or bell, the kind sounded in services during Holy Week: "Take this *tentennella*. Carry it with you always, sounding it to warn others of your presence."

It is now sunset, the hour when this service is customarily held. The cortege forms as if for a funeral, but instead of going to the cemetery, it moves into an adjoining wing and down a flight of steps into a half underground passage. The cell which is to be occupied by the leper has already been prepared and a wooden cross has been fastened to the door. Inside the cell is a low cot, like a coffin, a table, a chair, and a box. The leper is given sandals, a camelskin hood, an earthenware pot, a bowl made of beech wood to eat from, a copper jug, a belt, a knife. The leper is now required to make this response: "Here is my perpetual resting place. Here I shall live. This is my vow."

As the people silently leave, the door is shut. Outside the priest leaves an offering in a box provided for this purpose. The group returns to the chapel, where the priest concludes the service:

> Omnipotent God, who throws down the pride of the ancient enemy, through the sufferings of your only Son, give to your servant the necessary strength to bear with devotion and patience the evil that oppresses him. Amen.

5. Francis and the lepers. Painting by B. Berlinghieri (1228–1274).

This account of how lepers were received into hospitals in Francis's day actually applies only to the more fortunate ones. In contrast, the law of that time made unmistakably clear that anyone encountering a leper was free to kill him if he chose to do so, so great was the almost universal fear and dread of this disease, a fear and revulsion shared even by Francis himself as a young man.

* * *

Even today, if one follows the road leading from Assisi downward to the plain, reaches the church of Santa Maria degli Angeli and turns left following a narrow road southward, one comes upon a group of ruins in the fields, together with a small chapel surmounted by a belfry, set in their midst. A heavy mood of gloom pervades the place, even on the brightest of days. It is as though a melancholy atmosphere surrounds one in this desolate, lonely place, where on dark nights the wind occasionally causes the bell to sound a ghostly, sepulchral tone.

These are the ruins of one of eight leper hospitals maintained by the Comune of Assisi in the time of Francis. Originally called the hospital of San Lazzaro, named for the Lazarus who was "full of sores" in the parable in the Gospel of St. Luke, it was later renamed Santa Maria Maddelena.

Whenever Francis, dressed in his knightly regalia, the son of a wealthy merchant, a youth who loved life, a member of the Tripudianti who used to dance through the streets of Assisi at night, singing, bearing torches, wearing garlands, and enjoying festive banquets, whenever he rode along this road en route to one of his father's properties nearby, he always passed these hospital buildings with great fear and intense loathing. Although with averted face he tried to ride past the hospital quickly, he could not avoid seeing the poor emaciated figures, like the living dead, their eyes staring out of ashen faces, their disfigured bodies afflicted with oozing sores and even limbs partially rotted away. But worst of all was the all-pervading stench of putrefaction from the sores dripping with pus. Often he was moved to give money to the hospital, but always asked some one else to take it there because he could never bring himself to dismount from his horse anywhere near this dreaded place.

One day, as Francis was riding near this hospital on his way to one of his father's estates, his horse suddenly shied, and Francis saw that a man was standing directly in his path. Francis realized with horror that this man was a leper. Nevertheless, as though drawn by a power he could not resist, he dismounted, walked to the leper, took his leprous, blood-stained hand into his own. As he later recalled: "I felt as though I was grasping the hand of a corpse." As he half-consciously pressed a gold piece into the palm of this hand, he lifted his eyes and gazed fully into the man's face, disfigured by decaying sores, a face revolting and repulsive beyond measure, a visage of one of the most abject of all human creatures. As though he again was impelled by an invisible force beyond his conscious control, he embraced the man, kissing him on both cheeks and lips. As Francis' gaze fell to the ground, a great flood of spiritual emotion filled his entire being, an experience so overwhelming that he was to remember it to the very moment of his death. Silently the leper gently withdrew his hand. When Francis looked up, the leper was no longer there. He had vanished. Francis stood alone beside his horse. In describing this event, St. Bonaventure, one of the earliest biographers of Francis, stresses the fact that in this place there was absolutely nothing to obstruct the view, neither trees nor shrubs, only open fields stretching away into the distance.

After he had remounted his horse, it slowly began to dawn upon Francis that in the abject figure that stood before him, he had met the Christ. As with Saint Paul after Damascus, his whole world was transformed from that very moment. He had opened his heart to what, until then, he had rejected with utmost horror and revulsion. In that single instant a new quality was born in Francis, the quality of compassion. However, this was no weak, sentimental feeling, but a fully courageous Michaelic compassion, a knightly courage which filled Francis from that moment onward. Indeed, the time was to come when the first task assigned to anyone wishing to join the brotherhood was to live and work in the hospitals caring for the lepers, "the true Christians" as Francis called them. Even today, it remains a goal of those attempting to follow Saint Francis's example, to do everything possible to cleanse *all* human beings from their leprosy, because according to Francis every person is in reality a leper in the physical life, the soul life, the spiritual life. Thus in his last testament, written in the days preceding his death, looking back to the moment of this destiny-laden meeting, Francis recorded this event as the source of the inspiration for his entire life's work.

Not long after Francis's death, in the course of the thirteenth century, the pope granted many privileges to the leper hospital of San Lazzaro near Assisi. The papal documents by which these privileges were granted include words of profound historical and spiritual significance: "The leper hospital of San Lazzaro stands on the site where the Order of Saint Francis had its beginning. . . ."

Thus official recognition was given to the profound significance of the meeting between Francis and the leper on the road near this hospital, a meeting which laid the foundation for a rule of chivalry, involving bravery and valor far beyond that required by courageous knights in shining armor—the Rule of Compassion, which has its origin in an awakened human heart.

> Francis of Assisi made no attempt to set aside the experiences of the heart; on the contrary, he retained them in complete perfection. That is what is so grand and majestic about Francis of Assisi; he enlarged his heart to embrace his entire soul, his entire being.
>
> —Rudolf Steiner, Oslo, June 6, 1912

❧ 4 ❧

Francis of Assisi and the Creatures of the Earth

Without doubt, the quality that has endeared Francis of Assisi to untold numbers of people throughout the centuries from his own time to ours, is his unwavering love and concern for nature and for all creatures of the earth. By example, he inspired others to cherish and care for all earthly creation as the visible fruit of God's handiwork. He taught others that above all, joy must fill their life on earth, in contrast to the prevailing attitude up to his time, which considered earthly existence as life spent only in a dark valley of shadow, a place of tears filled with suffering and sadness from which one longed to escape. This attitude was exacerbated by the terrible human misdeeds against the earth, its creatures, and against each other everywhere.

In contrast, Francis regarded earthly life as possessing ideal, positive potential as God's creation. Thus Francis clearly showed himself to be what Rudolf Steiner once characterized as "the first materialist" in the best sense of the word. This point of view is further reflected in the words of a very wise man who once said: "Matter is not *what* we see, it is the *way* we see God's creation." Indeed, for people everywhere, it is this power of simultaneously seeing and being that epitomizes the life and work of Francis of Assisi.

In order to illustrate this profoundly unique relationship between Francis and all creation, the following examples have been selected from the writings of the early Franciscan chroniclers concerning events of his life, and above all from that incomparable spiritual gem; *The Little Flowers of St. Francis (I Fioretti)*. These clearly show Francis not only as one of the greatest lovers of nature, but amply justify his designation in our time as the patron saint of ecology.

*   *   *

Thomas of Celano, the earliest biographer of Francis, in his *First Life of Francis of Assisi*, gives a moving firsthand impression of the Poverello's great love for all creation:

Who could ever give expression to the very great affection he bore for all things that are God's? Who would be able to narrate the sweetness he enjoyed while contemplating in creatures the wisdom of their creator, his power and his goodness? Indeed, he was very often filled with a wonderful and ineffable joy from this consideration while he looked upon the sun, while he beheld the moon, and while he gazed upon the stars and the firmament. O simple piety and pious simplicity! Even toward little worms he glowed with a very great love, for he had read this saying about the Savior: "I am a worm, not a man." Therefore he picked them up from the road and placed them in a safe place, lest they be crushed by the feet of the passersby. What shall I say of the lower creatures, when he would see to it that the bees would be provided with honey in the winter, or the best wine, lest they should die from the cold? He used to praise in particular the perfection of their works and the excellence of their skill, for the glory of God, with such encomiums that he would often spend a whole day in praising them and the rest of God's creatures. For as of old the three youths in the fiery furnace invited all the elements to praise and glorify the creator of the universe, so also this man, filled with the spirit of God, never ceased to glorify, praise, and bless the creator and ruler of all things in all the elements and creatures.

How great a gladness do you think the beauty of the flowers brought to his mind when he saw the shape of their beauty and perceived the odor of their sweetness? He used to turn the eye of consideration immediately to the beauty of that flower that comes from "the root of Jesse" and gives light in the days of spring and by its fragrance has raised innumerable thousands from the dead. When he found an abundance of flowers, he preached to them and invited them to praise the Lord as though they were endowed with reason. In the same way he exhorted with the sincerest purity cornfields and vineyards, stones and forests, and all the beautiful things of the fields, fountains of water and the green things of the gardens, earth and fire, air and wind, to love God and serve him willingly. Finally, he called all creatures Brother, and in a most extraordinary manner, a manner never experienced by others, he discerned the hidden things of nature with his sensitive heart, as one who had already escaped *"into the freedom of the glory of the sons of God."*

.   .   .

Above all creatures unendowed with reason he had a particular love of the sun and for fire. He used to say, "At dawn, when the sun rises, all men should praise God, who created him for our use, and through him gives light to our eyes by day. And at nightfall every man should praise God for Brother Fire, by whom he gives light to our eyes in the darkness. For we are all blind, and by these two brothers of ours, God gives light to our eyes, so we should give special praise to our creator for these and other creatures that serve us day by day."

Next to fire he had a special love for water, because it symbolizes holy penitence and tribulation, and at Baptism the soul is cleansed from its stains and receives its first purification. So whenever he washed his hands, he chose a place where the water would not be trodden underfoot as it fell to the ground. For the same reason, whenever he had to walk over rocks, he trod reverently and fearfully, out of love for Christ who is called The Rock. Whenever he recited the psalm, "Thou wilt set me high up on a rock," he used to say with great reverence and devotion, "Thou hast set me up at the foot of the rock."

He told the friar who cut and chopped wood for the fire, that he must never cut down the whole tree, but remove branches in such a way that a part of the tree remained intact, out of love for Christ, who willed to accomplish our salvation on the wood of the cross.

In the same way he told the friar who cared for the gardens not to cultivate all the ground for vegetables, but to set aside a plot to grow flowers to bloom in their season, out of love for him who is called "the rose on the plain and the lily on the mountain slopes." Indeed, he told the brother-gardener that he should always make a pleasant flower garden, and cultivate every variety of fragrant herb and flowering plant, so that all who saw the herbs and flowers would be moved to praise God. For every creature proclaims, "God made me for your sake, O mortal."

Indeed, Francis took inward and outward delight in almost every creature. When he handled or looked at them, his spirit seemed to be in heaven rather than on earth. And not long before his death, in gratitude for the many consolations that he had received through creatures, he composed "The Praises of the Lord in his Creatures," in order to stir the hearts of those who heard them to the praise of God, and to move humans to praise the Lord in his creatures.

·   ·   ·

In his *Second Life of Francis of Assisi,* Thomas of Celano gives a vivid picture of Francis's power over the forces of nature expressed in the changes of weather, wild beasts, and fire:

> Francis liked to stay at the brother's place at Greccio, both because he saw that it was rich by reason of its poverty and because there he could surrender himself more freely to heavenly things in a secluded cell hewn from a projecting rock. This was the place where he brought back to memory the birthday of the child of Bethlehem, becoming a child with that child. It happened, however, that the inhabitants were being annoyed by many evils, for a pack of ravening wolves was devouring not only the animals but even human beings. Every year hailstorms were devastating the fields and vineyards. One day, when he was preaching to them, Francis said: "To the honor and glory of almighty God, hear the truth I announce to you. If every one of you confesses his sins and brings forth fruits befitting repentance, I give you my word that every pestilence will depart and the Lord, looking kindly upon you, will grant you an increase of temporal goods. But hear this also: again I announce to you that if you are ungrateful for his gifts and return to your vomit, the plague will be renewed, your punishment will be doubled, and even greater wrath will be let loose upon you."
>
> It happened, therefore, by the merits and prayers of the holy father, that from that hour the destruction ceased, the dangers passed, and neither the wolves nor the hailstorms caused any further damage. Moreover, what is greater still, if any hail came down over the fields of their neighbors, it either stopped short when it got near the border of their lands or turned aside to some other region.

·   ·   ·

Thomas of Celano also recalled that:

> It is not surprising that fire and other creatures sometimes showed respect for him. In fact, we who lived with him were witnesses of his affection and respect for them and of the pleasure they gave him. He had so much love and sympathy for them that he was disturbed when they were treated without respect. He spoke to them with a great inner and outer joy, as if they had been endowed by God with feeling, intelligence, and speech. Very often it was for him the occasion to become enraptured in God.
>
> One day when he was seated near the hearth, his linen underclothes caught fire the whole length of his leg without his being aware of it. He felt the heat, but when one of his companions saw that his clothes were burning and hurried to extinguish them, he said to him: "No, my dearest brother, don't harm our Brother Fire." He did not let him put it out. The brother ran to find blessed Francis's brother guardian and lead him to the place. They extinguished the flames, but against Francis's will. He did not even want them to extinguish a candle, a lamp, or fire, as one does when it is no longer needed, so great was his tenderness and pity for that creature. He also forbade the brothers to throw embers or half-burned logs to the winds, as is customarily done: he wanted them to be placed gently on the ground out of respect for him who had created them.

·   ·   ·

In *The Little Flowers of St. Francis* is told the story of the miraculous multiplication of the fruits from the ruined vineyard of the priest at Rieti:

> When he arrived near Rieti, such a great crowd of people came out to meet him that he therefore did not want to go into the city, but turned aside and went to a certain church that was about two miles away from the town. But the people, knowing that he was staying at that church, flocked out to see him in such throngs that the vineyard of the priest of that church—for it was vintage time— was completely ruined and all the grapes were taken and eaten. When the priest saw the damage, he was bitterly sorry and he regretted that he had allowed St. Francis to go into his church.

The priest's thoughts were revealed to the saint by the Holy Spirit, and he summoned the priest and said to him: "My dear Father, how many measures of wine does this vineyard produce in a year when it produces well?"

The priest answered: "Twelve."

St. Francis said: "Then I beg of you, Father, to bear patiently my staying here in this church of yours for some days, because of the rest and quiet that I find here. And let everyone take the grapes from this vineyard of yours, for the love of God and my poor little self. And I promise you on behalf of my Lord Jesus Christ that this year you will get twenty measures."

St. Francis did this—staying on there—because of the great good that he saw the Lord was performing in the souls of the people who came there, for he saw that many of them, when they went away, were inebriated with the love of God and were converted to heavenly longings, forgetting the world. Therefore, it seemed to him better that the material vineyard should be damaged than that the vineyard of the Lord of Hosts should be sterile in heavenly wine.

So the priest trusted in the promise of St. Francis and freely let the people who came there take and eat the grapes. It certainly is a wonderful thing that although the vineyard was completely stripped and ruined by them, so that only a few little bunches of grapes remained, when the vintage came, the priest trusting in the Saint's promise, gathered those little bunches of grapes and put them in the wine press and pressed them. And as St. Francis had promised, he obtained twenty measures of the very best wine that year.

By that miracle it was clearly shown that, just as through the merits of St. Francis the vineyard with its ruined grapes had produced an abundance of wine, so the Christian people, who were sterile in virtue because of sin, through the merits and teaching of St. Francis frequently brought forth good fruits of penance.

*   *   *

Two charming, unforgettable illustrations of Francis' love for the creatures of the insect world have been preserved in the *Second Life* by Thomas of Celano:

Near the cell of the saint of God at the Porziuncula, there was a tree cricket that used to perch on a fig tree and frequently sing sweetly. At times the blessed father would extend his hand to it and kindly call it to himself, saying: "My sister cricket, come to me." As though endowed with reason, it immediately got up on his hand. And Francis said to it, "Sing my sister cricket, and praise your creator with a joyful song." Obeying without delay, it began to sing, and it did not cease until the man of God, mingling his own praises with its songs, commanded it to go back to its usual haunt. It remained there for eight days in a row, as if bound there. But when the saint would come down from his cell, he would always touch it with his hands and command it to sing, and it was always ready to obey his commands. And the saint said to his companions: "Let us give our sister cricket leave to go now, for she has made us sufficiently happy; we do not want our flesh to rejoice vainly over things of this kind." And immediately with permission from Francis, the cricket left, and it never returned there again. Seeing all these things, the brothers were greatly astonished.

·　·　·

On a certain mountain, a cell was once constructed in which the servant of God performed penance most strictly for forty days. When this space of time was completed, he left the place and the cell remained without another inhabitant after him, placed as it was in a lonely spot. An earthen vessel, from which the saint used to drink, was also abandoned there. Once, however, when some men went to that place out of reverence for the saint, they found the vessel filled with bees. They had built little cells in the vessel with wonderful skill, signifying, surely, the sweetness of the contemplation that the saint had experienced there.

·　·　·

According to an ancient Hebrew tradition, the only creatures that escaped the fall of man and nature in the Garden of Eden were the fish. For this reason, the fish became one of the earliest Christian symbols to represent the Christ. Doubtless, Francis knew of this tradition, and Thomas of Celano recorded the following:

Francis was moved by a tender affection toward fish, which, when they were caught, and he had the chance, he threw back into the water, commanding them to be careful lest they be caught again.

Once when he was sitting in a boat near a port in the lake of Rieti, a certain fisherman, who had caught a big fish popularly, called a *tinca* offered it kindly to him. He accepted it joyfully and kindly, and began to call it Brother. Then placing it in the water outside the boat, he began devoutly to bless the name of the Lord. While he continued in prayer for some time, the fish played in the water beside the boat and did not go away from the place where it had been put, until his prayers was finished and the holy man of God gave it permission to leave.

* * *

One of the most faithful followers of Francis of Assisi was Anthony of Padova. The following extraordinary account of his preaching to the fishes is included in the *The Little Flowers of St. Francis*. It illustrates his faithfulness to the spirit of Francis's love toward all creatures:

Once when St. Anthony was in Rimini, where there were many heretics, wishing to lead them back to the light of the true faith and onto the path of truth, he preached to them for many days and argued about the faith of Christ and about Holy Scripture. But they were stubborn and hardhearted, and not only did they not accept his holy teaching, but, moreover, they refused to listen to him.

So one day, by an inspiration from God, St. Anthony went to the mouth of the river near the sea. And standing on the bank between the sea and the river, he began to call the fishes in God's name, as for a sermon, saying: "You fishes of the sea and river, listen to the word of God, since the faithless heretics refuse to hear it!"

As soon as he said this, all of a sudden such a great throng of large and small fishes gathered before him near the bank as had never been seen in that sea or river. And all of them held their heads a bit out of the water, gazing intently at St. Anthony's face. There you would have seen the big fishes staying close to the little ones, while the smaller ones peacefully swam or stayed under the fins of the larger fishes. You would also have seen the different types of fishes hasten to group themselves together and range themselves before the saint's face, like a field painted and adorned with a marvelous variety of colors. You would have seen schools of big fishes occupy the distant places in order to hear the sermon, like an army ranged for battle. You would have seen the middle-sized fishes take their positions in the center and stay there without any disturbance, as though they were instructed by God. And you would have seen a great and very dense crowd of small fishes come in a hurry, like pilgrims going to receive an indulgence, and approach closer to the holy father as if to their protector. And so first the smaller fishes near the bank, secondly the middle-sized, and thirdly the largest fishes, where the water was deeper, attended this divinely arranged sermon of St. Anthony—all in very great peace and meekness and order.

Then when all the fishes were in their place in perfect order, St. Anthony solemnly began to preach, saying:

"My fish brothers, you should give as many thanks as you can to your creator who has granted you such a noble element as your dwelling place, so that you have fresh and salt water, just as you please. Moreover he has given you many refuges to escape from storms. He has also given you a clear and transparent element, and ways to travel and food to live on. Your kind creator also prepares for you the food that you need, even in the depths of the ocean. When he created you at the creation of the world, he gave you the command to increase and multiply, and he gave you his blessing. Later during the flood, when all the other animals were perishing, God preserved you alone without loss. He has also given you fins so that without additional power, you can roam wherever you wish. It was granted to you, by order of God, to keep alive Jonah, the prophet of the Lord, and to cast him onto dry land safe and sound on the third day. You offered the tribute money to our Lord Jesus Christ, when as a poor man He had nothing to pay the tax. You were chosen as food for the eternal king, our Blessed Lord Jesus Christ, before his resurrection and in a mysterious way afterwards. Because of all these things you should praise and bless the lord, who has given you so many more blessings than to other creatures."

At these and similar words and preaching of St. Anthony, some of the fishes began to open their mouths, and all of them nodded their heads, and by these and other signs of reverence they praised God as much as they could.

Then St. Anthony, seeing how reverent the fishes were toward God the creator, rejoiced in spirit and cried out in a loud voice: "Blessed be the eternal God because the fishes of the waters give God more honor than heretical men, and animals lacking reason listen to his word better than faithless men!"

And the longer St. Anthony preached, the more the throng of fishes increased, and not one of them left the place it had taken.

At this miracle the people of the city, including the above-mentioned heretics, came running. And when they saw the marvelous and extraordinary miracle of the fishes listening to St. Anthony, all of them felt remorse in their hearts. They sat down at his feet so that he could preach a sermon to them.

Then St. Anthony preached so wonderfully about the Catholic religion that he converted and brought to the true faith of Christ all those heretics who were there, and the faithful he sent home with his blessing, strengthened in their faith and filled with joy.

St. Anthony also dismissed the fishes with God's blessing, and they all swam away to various parts of the sea, rejoicing and expressing their joy and applause in amazing games and gambols.

After this, St. Anthony stayed in Rimini for many days, preaching and reaping much spiritual fruit, both by converting heretics and by stimulating the piety of the clergy.

*   *   *

Probably the best known of all the stories about Francis of Assisi and the creatures of nature is represented in the almost universally known painting by Giotto, in the upper church of the Basilica di San Francesco in Assisi: "St. Francis Preaching to the Birds." The following report of this event is taken from the *First Life of St. Francis* by Thomas of Celano, and is accompanied by accounts of other incidents of a similar nature taken from contemporary sources:

> Francis came to a certain place near Bevagna where a very great number of birds of various kinds had congregated—namely, doves, crows, and some others popularly called daws. When the most blessed servant of God, Francis, saw them, being a man of very great fervor and great tenderness toward lower creatures, he left his companions in the road and ran eagerly toward the birds. When he was close enough to them, seeing that they were waiting expect-

antly for him, he greeted them in his usual way. Not a little sur-
prised that the birds did not rise in flight, as they usually do, he
was filled with great joy and humbly begged them to listen to the
word of God. Among the many things he spoke to them were these
words "My brothers, birds, you should praise your creator very much
and always love him; he gave you feathers to clothe you, wings so
that you can fly, and whatever else was necessary for you. God
made you noble among his creatures, and he gave you a home in the
purity of the air; though you neither sow nor reap, he nevertheless
protects and governs you without any solicitude on your part." At
these words, as Francis himself used to say and those too who were
with him, the birds, rejoicing in a wonderful way according to their
nature, began to stretch their necks, extend their wings, open their
mouths, and gaze at him. And Francis, passing through their midst,
went on his way and returned, touching their heads and bodies
with his tunic. Finally he blessed them, and then, after he had
made the sign of the cross over them, he gave them permission to
fly away to some other place. Francis went his way with his companions, rejoicing and giving thanks to God, whom all creatures vener-
ate with humble acknowledgment. But now that he had become
simple by grace, not by nature, he began to blame himself for
negligence in not having preached to the birds before, seeing that
they had listened to the word of God with such great reverence.
And so it happened that, from that day on, he solicitously admon-
ished all birds, all animals and reptiles, and even creatures that
have no feeling, to praise and love their creator daily, when the
name of the savior has been invoked, for he saw their obedience
by personal experience.

.   .   .

When the blessed Francis was going across the lake of Rieti to the
hermitage of Greccio, he was sitting in a little boat, when a certain
fisherman offered him a waterfowl, that he might rejoice over it in
the Lord. The blessed father accepted it joyfully, and opening his
hands, he gently told it that it was free to fly away. But when it
did not wish to leave, but wanted to rest there in his hands as in
a nest, the saint raised his eyes and remained in prayer. And returning to himself as from another place after a long while, he
gently commanded the bird to go back to its former freedom. So,

6.
Francis preaching to the birds.
Fresco by Giotto (1267–1337).
Upper church, Basilica of
San Francesco, Assisi.
(*Scala, Florence, Italy.*)

7.
Francis and the turtle dove.
Drawing by E. Burnand.
(*Facchinetti, San Francesco
d'Assisi, p. 372.*)

upon receiving this permission along with a blessing, the bird joyfully flew away.

.   .   .

A certain nobleman from the Comune of Sienna sent a pheasant to the blessed Francis while the latter was ill. He accepted it with alacrity, not with the desire of eating it, but in the way he always rejoiced over such things, out of love for the creator. And he said to the pheasant: "May our creator be praised, brother pheasant!" And to the brothers he said: "Let us see now if brother pheasant will stay with us, or if it will go back to its usual and more suitable haunt." One of the brothers took it, at the command of the saint, and placed it at a distance in the vineyard. Immediately, however, it came directly back to the father's cell. Again, Francis ordered it placed even farther away; but it came back with the greatest speed to the door of his cell and entered almost by force under the habit of the brother who was standing at the door. The saint then ordered it to be fed diligently, embracing it and caressing it with soft words. When a certain physician who was quite devoted to the saint of God saw this, he begged the pheasant from the brothers, not wanting to eat it, but to raise it out of reverence for the saint. He took it home with him; but the pheasant, as though it had suffered an injury in being separated from the saint, refused to eat as long as it was away from Francis's presence. The physician was astonished, and immediately took the pheasant back to the saint. He told him everything just as it had happened. As soon as the pheasant was put upon the ground, it saw its father, and putting off all grief, it began to eat with joy.

.   .   .

One day the blessed Francis was sitting at the table with his brothers. Two little birds, one male, the other female, came up, and, solicitous about the bringing up of their newly born little ones, they took the crumbs from the table of the saint as they pleased and as they had been doing day by day. The holy man rejoiced in creatures like these and he coaxed them, as was his custom, and offered them grain solicitously. One day the father and the mother offered their little ones to the brothers, as having being reared at their expense, and after they had given their little ones to the brothers, they did not appear in that place again. The little birds grew tame among the brothers and perched on their hands, not indeed as guests, but as belonging to that house. They avoided the sight of secular people and professed themselves foster children only of their brothers. The saint observed this and was astonished, and he invited the brothers to rejoice. "See," he said, "what our brothers with the red breasts do, as though they were endowed with reason. For they have said: "Behold, brothers, we present to you our little ones who have been nourished with your crumbs, do with them as you wish, for we are going to another home." They became completely tame among the brothers and took their food together with them. But later, greed broke up the peace, in that the greed of the larger bird persecuted the small ones. For when the bigger one had had his fill, as he wished, he drove the rest away from the food. "See," said the father, "see what this greedy one is doing. Even though he is full and satisfied, he envies his hungry brothers. He will come to a bad end yet." The revenge followed quickly upon the words of the saint. The disturber of his brothers got up on a vessel of water to drink and immediately fell into the water and suffocating, died. No cat was found nor any beast that would touch the bird that had been cursed by the saint.

· · ·

Though the crow, black and frightening, is the antithesis of the dove, Francis's crow, thanks to his master, went to choir with the brothers, ate with them in the refectory, and visited the sick in the infirmary of the friary. He also went with them to Assisi's houses to beg for alms. When Francis died, the crow languished and would take no food. He refused to leave Francis's tomb and died there from grief and weakness.

· · ·

One time, when Francis was walking with another friar in the Venetian marshes, they came upon a huge flock of birds, singing among the reeds. When he saw them, the saint said to his companion, "Our sisters the birds are praising their creator. We will go in among them and sing God's praise, chanting the divine office." They went in among the birds which remained where they were, so that the friars couldn't hear themselves saying the office, they were making so much noise. Eventually the saint turned to them and said, "My sisters, stop singing until we have given God the praise to which he has a right." The birds were silent immediately and remained that way until Francis gave them permission to sing again, after they had take plenty of time to say the office and had finished their praises. Then the birds began again, as usual.

· · ·

A boy of the town of Sienna caught a number of turtledoves in a snare, and he was carrying them to the market to sell them. But St. Francis, who was always very kind and wonderfully compassionate, especially toward gentle animals and little birds, was stirred by love and pity on seeing the doves. And he said to the boy who was carrying them: "Good boy, please give me those doves so that such innocent birds, which in Holy Scripture are symbols of pure, humble, and faithful souls, will not fall into the hands of cruel men who will kill them."

The boy was then inspired by God to give all the doves to St. Francis. When the kind father had gathered them to his bosom, he began to talk to them in a very gentle way, saying: "My simple, chaste, and innocent sister doves, why did you let yourselves be caught? I want to rescue you from death and make nests for you where you can lay your eggs and fulfill the creator's commandment to multiply."

St. Francis took them with him and made a nest for all of them. And the doves settled in the nests made by St. Francis, and laid their eggs and reared their young right among the friars, and they increased in numbers. They were so tame and familiar with St. Francis and the other friars that they seemed to be like chickens that had always been raised by the friars. And they did not leave until St. Francis gave them permission, with his blessing.

The saint had said to the boy who gave him the doves: "My son, one day you will become a Friar Minor in this order, and you will serve Our Lord Jesus Christ well." And it happened as the saint foretold, because later the boy entered the order and through the merits of St. Francis, he led a praiseworthy and very exemplary life until he died. So St. Francis not only obtained comfort for those little birds in this life but also the joys of eternal life for that youth.

· · ·

The humility and innocence of the lamb is often cited in connection with the nature of Francis of Assisi himself, who saw in these gentle creatures an earthly symbol of Christ, the Lamb of God. The following extracts tell about lambs and other animals, because in Francis's eyes

7 A. Woodcut of Francis and the Wolf.

8.
The people of Gubbio feeding the tamed wolf. Drawing by E. Burnand. (*Facchinetti, San Francesco d'Assisi, p. 354.*)

all creatures are entitled to man's love and concern as creations of God. Among these are stories of the deer, the ass, the rabbit, and finally, perhaps the most famous "animal story" connected with Francis of Assisi, that of the "Wolf of Gubbio":

> When he was passing through the marches, with the same brother serving gladly as his companion, he met a certain man who had two little lambs hanging bound over his shoulder, taking them to the market to sell them. When blessed Francis heard them bleating, he was filled with pity. Coming close, he touched them and showed his compassion for them like a mother over her weeping child. And he said to the man: "Why are you torturing my brother lambs tied up and hanging like this?" Answering, he said; "I am taking them to the market to sell them, because I need the money." The saint said: "What will happen to them then?" He answered: "Those who buy them, will kill them and eat them." "God forbid," replied the saint; "this must not happen. Take the mantle I am wearing as their price and give the lambs to me." He quickly gave him the lambs and took the mantle, for the mantel was of much greater value. Now the saint had borrowed the mantle that day from a certain faithful man to ward off the cold. The saint, after receiving the lambs, considered carefully what he should do with them, and, at the advice of his companion, he gave them to that man who had lent him the mantle, asking him to care for them. He commanded him not to sell them at any time, or to do them any harm, but to keep them, feed them, and take care of them conscientiously.

> • • •

> While in Rome, St. Francis had a lamb with him which he kept out of reverence for the Lamb of God; and when he was leaving, he gave it to Lady Jacoba di Settesoli to keep. The lamb accompanied its mistress to church and stayed there with her, refusing to leave until she left, just as if the saint had trained it to do this. When she was late getting up in the morning, the lamb nudged her with its horns and roused her with its bleats, urging her to hurry and go to church. She was amazed and became very fond of the animal that had been a disciple of St. Francis and was now a "master" of the religious life.

> • • •

> Saint Francis had power not only over men, but also over the fishes of the sea, the birds of the air, and the beasts of the field. For it is

said of him that when he was once going from place to place and his path lay through a certain wood, the deer fled from him and his companion. To one of them therefore, the saint cried: "Why do you run away? Stand still." And at the word of the saint the stag stood still, and Francis went up and put his hands upon him, and said: "Now go, and praise God."

* * *

Brother Tebaldo once told something he himself had seen. When Saint Francis was preaching one day to the people of Trevi, a noisy and ungovernable ass went careering about the square, frightening the people out of their wits. And when it became clear that no one could catch or restrain him, Saint Francis said to him: "Brother ass, please be quiet and allow me to preach to the people." When the donkey heard this, he immediately bowed his head and, to everyone's astonishment, stood perfectly quiet. And the blessed Francis, fearing that the people might take too much notice of this astonishing miracle, began saying funny things to make them laugh.

* * *

Once when he was staying at the town of Greccio, a little rabbit that had been caught in a trap was brought alive to him by a certain brother. When the most blessed man saw it, he was moved to pity and said: "Brother rabbit, come to me. Why did you allow yourself to be caught like this?" And as soon as the rabbit had been let go by the brother who held it, it hopped to the saint, and, without being forced by anyone, it lay quiet in his bosom as the safest place possible. After it had rested there a little while, the holy father, caressing it with motherly affection, released it so it could return free to the woods. But when it had been placed upon the ground several times and had returned each time to the Saint's bosom, he finally commanded it be carried by the bothers to the nearby woods.

* * *

At a time when Saint Francis was staying in the mountain town of Gubbio, something wonderful and worthy of lasting fame happened.

There appeared near the city a fearfully large and fierce wolf which was so rabid with hunger that it devoured not only animals but even human beings. All the people in the town considered it such a great scourge and terror—because it often came near the town—that they took weapons with them when they went into the country, as if they were going to war. But even with their weapons they were not able to escape the sharp teeth and raging hunger of the wolf when they were so unfortunate as to meet it. Consequently, everyone in the town was so terrified that hardly anyone dared go outside the city gate.

But God wished to bring the holiness of Saint Francis to the attention of those people. For while the Saint was there at that time, he had pity on the people and decided to go out and meet the wolf. On hearing this the citizens said to him: "Look out, Brother Francis. Don't go outside the gate, because the wolf which has already devoured many people will certainly attack you and kill you!"

But Saint Francis placed his trust in the Lord Jesus Christ who is master of all creatures. Protected not by a shield or a helmet, but arming himself with the sign of the cross, he bravely went out of the town with his companions, putting all his faith in the Lord who makes those who believe in him walk without any injury on an asp and a basilisk, and trample not merely on a wolf but even on a lion or a dragon. With this very great faith, Saint Francis bravely went out to meet the wolf.

Some peasants accompanied him a little way, but soon they said to him: "We don't want to go any further because the wolf is very fierce and we might get hurt." When he heard them say this, St. Francis answered: "Just stay here. But I am going on to where the wolf lives."

Then, in the sight of many people who had come out and climbed onto high places to see this wonderful event, the fierce wolf came running toward St. Francis and his companions with its mouth open. The saint made the sign of the cross toward it. And the power of God checked the wolf, and made it slow down and close its cruel mouth.

Then calling to it, St. Francis said: "Come to me, Brother Wolf. In the name of Christ, I order you not to hurt me or anyone." It is marvelous to relate that as soon as he had made the sign of the cross, the wolf closed its terrible jaws and stopped running. As soon as he gave it that order, it lowered its head and lay down at the saint's feet, as though it had become a lamb.

Saint Francis said to it as it lay in front of him: "Brother Wolf, you have done great harm in this place, and you have committed horrible crimes by destroying God's creatures without any mercy. You have been destroying not only animals, but you even have the more detestable brazenness to kill and devour human beings made in the image of God. You therefore deserve to be put to death just like the worst robber and murderer. Consequently everyone is right in crying out against you and complaining, and this whole town is your enemy. But, Brother Wolf, I want to make peace between you and them, so that they will not be harmed by you any more, and after they have forgiven you for all your past crimes, neither men nor dogs will pursue you any longer."

The wolf showed by moving its body and tail and ears and by nodding its head that it willingly accepted what the saint had said and would observe it. So Saint Francis spoke again: "Brother Wolf, since you are willing to make and keep this peace pact, I promise you that I will have the people of this town give you food every day as long as you live, so that you will never again suffer from hunger, for I know that whatever evil you have been doing was done because of the pangs of hunger. But my Brother Wolf, since I am obtaining such a favor for you, I want you to promise me that you will never hurt any animal or man again. Will you promise me this?" The wolf gave a clear sign, by nodding its head, that it promised to do what the saint asked.

And Saint Francis said: "Brother Wolf, I want you to give me a pledge so that I can confidently believe what you promise." As Saint Francis held out his hand to receive the pledge, the wolf also raised its front paw and meekly and gently put it in St. Francis's hand as a sign that it was giving its pledge. Then Saint Francis said: "Brother Wolf, I order you, in the name of the Lord Jesus Christ, to come with me now, without fear, into the town to make this peace pact in the name of the Lord." The wolf immediately began to walk alongside Saint Francis, just like a very gentle lamb. When the people saw this, they were greatly amazed. The news spread quickly through the whole town, so that all of them, men as well as women, great and small, assembled in the marketplace, because Saint Francis was there with the wolf.

When a very large crowd had gathered, Saint Francis gave them a wonderful sermon, saying among other things, that such calamities were permitted by God because of their sins, and how the consuming fire of hell by which the damned have to be devoured for all eternity is much more dangerous than the raging of a wolf, which can kill nothing but the body. How much more they should fear to be plunged into hell, since one little animal could keep so great a crowd in such a state of terror and trembling. "So dear people," he said "come back to the Lord, and do fitting penance, and God will free you from the wolf in this world and from the devouring fire of hell in the next." And having said this, he added: "Listen dear people. Brother Wolf, who is standing here before you, has promised me and has given me a pledge that he will make peace with you and will never hurt you if you promise to feed him every day. And I pledge myself as bondsman for Brother Wolf that he will faithfully keep this peace pact."

Then all the people who were assembled there promised in a loud voice to feed the wolf regularly. And St. Francis said to the wolf before all of them: "And you, Brother Wolf, do you promise to keep this pact, that is not to hurt any animal or human being?" The wolf knelt down and bowed its head, and by moving its body and wagging its tail and ears it clearly showed to everyone that it would keep the pact as it had promised. And Saint Francis said: "Brother Wolf, just as you gave me a pledge of this when we were outside the city gate, I want you to give me a pledge here before all these people that you will keep the pact and will never betray me for having pledged myself as your bondsman." Then in the presence of all the people, the wolf raised its right paw and put it in St. Francis's hand as a pledge.

The crowd was so filled with amazement and joy, out of devotion for the saint as well as over the novelty of the miracle and over the peace pact between the wolf and themselves, that they all shouted out to the sky, praising and blessing the Lord Jesus Christ who had sent Saint Francis to them. By his merits they had been freed from such a fierce wolf, and saved from such a terrible scourge and had recovered peace and quiet.

From that day onward, the wolf and the people kept the pact that St. Francis made. The wolf lived for some years more, and it went from door to door for food. It hurt no one, and no one hurt it. The people fed it courteously, and it is a striking fact that not a single dog barked at it. Then the wolf grew old and died. And the people were sorry, because whenever it went through the town, its peaceful kindness and patience reminded them of the virtues and the holiness of Saint Francis.

This account from the twenty-first chapter of the *Fioretti*, of St. Francis taming the Wolf of Gubbio, received some further authenticity a few years ago. The skeleton of a wolf was found buried near the altar under the floor of the church of San Francesco della Pace at Gubbio.

9. Cover illustration from the early-nineteenth-century German edition of "The Little Flowers of St. Francis."

❧ 5 ❧

The Mountain Aflame

Medieval literature abounds in many examples of highly significant dreams and visions. In connection with the individuality of Francis of Assisi, one of the most remarkable dreams is that of Silvestro, a canon of the cathedral of San Rufino. In Spring 1209, he experienced a vision three times in succession. He was so overcome by what he had seen that he went to Francis and told him and the companions about it. In the third chapter of the Major Life of Saint Francis by St. Bonaventure, this episode is described:

> At first when Father Silvestro saw the way Francis and his friars were behaving, he looked on it in a purely human fashion and he was disgusted, but then God visited him with his grace in order to save him from his rash temerity. He had a dream in which he saw the whole of Assisi caught in the coils of a huge dragon, which threatened to devastate the entire city by its sheer size. (This dragon is similar to the one described by the Old Testament prophet Daniel, a terrible creature raging through the city of Babylon, a city which was permeated by every kind of sin against God.) Father Silvestro saw a cross of gold coming from Francis' mouth; the top of it reached up to heaven and its arms stretched far and wide, seeming to embrace the whole earth. The dragon was entirely vanquished at the sight of the golden cross. Father Silvestro realized that the vision was a revelation from God; and after he had seen it for the third time, he told Saint Francis and his friars all about it. A short time afterwards he joined Francis and followed in the footsteps of Christ with such perseverance that his life in the

Order only served to confirm the vision that he had seen while in
the world.

St. Bonaventure goes on to relate the effect this vision had on
Francis of Assisi:

> St. Francis refused to be carried away with worldly pride when he
> heard about the vision. He acknowledged God's goodness in the
> gifts he bestows and became more eager than ever to put the
> dragon-enemy of the human race to flight with all its cunning, and
> to proclaim the glory of Christ's Cross. One day when he was in a
> lonely place by himself, the joy of the Holy Spirit was infused into
> him and he was assured that his sins had all been forgiven. He was
> rapt in ecstasy and completely absorbed in a wonderful light, so
> that the depths of his soul were illuminated and he saw what the
> future held in store for himself and his brothers. Then he returned
> to the friars once again and told them, "Have courage, my dearly
> beloved, and rejoice in God. There is no need to be distressed
> because there are only a few of us, nor any need to be afraid because
> we have no experience. God has shown me beyond all shadow of
> doubt that he will make us grow into a great multitude and that
> the order will spread far and wide by favor of His blessing."

Implicit in the dream of Father Silvestro is one of the oldest and
most significant cosmic pictures known to humanity, not only during
the Middle Ages but extending back to the earliest times of humanity's
life on earth. Depicted in many guises, it appears in the mythology of
ancient India, Persia, Egypt, and Chaldea, finally attaining a kind of
fulfillment in Christian times in the representation of the battle between the Archangel Michael and the dragon. In ancient Hebrew
writings a similar struggle was depicted in the figure of the serpent in
the Garden of Eden, and culminated in the image of the awesome,
terrifying dragon appearing in the apocalyptic Book of Revelation of
Saint John.

Traditionally, the annual Christian festival of Michaelmas occurs at
the end of September, after the autumn equinox. The autumnal mood
of this season of the year calls forth the mighty image of Michael's
battle with the dragon, and the tension between the decreasing light
and the increasing darkness as expressed in outer nature. In the periodi-

10. Francis calling forth water from the rocks during the ascent of Mount La Verna. Fresco by Giotto, upper church, Basilica of San Francesco, Assisi. (*Scala, Florence, Italy.*)

cal *Das Goetheanum* of September 30, 1923, an essay was published, "Michael and the Dragon," written by Rudolf Steiner, in which the following appears:

> The leaves fall from the trees, all the flowering and fruiting life of the plants dies away. In gentle, friendly guise, nature receives man in spring, cherishes him through the long summer days, nurturing him with the warmth-laden gifts of the sun. When autumn comes, nature has nothing more to give him. The forces of decay press in upon him and through his senses he beholds them in pictures. Out of his own being man must give himself what hitherto nature has given him. Out of the spiritual world he must create forces for himself that will be able to help where nature fails. The picture of Michael rises up within him, Michael the opponent of the dragon. . . . Nor must we think of it merely as a picture, for it is a reality for the soul. It is as if the warmth of summer had dropped a curtain before the spiritual world, and with the coming of autumn this curtain is now lifted. With such thoughts and feelings men of ancient times kept the festival of Michael in their hearts.

The time of Michaelmas 1224 was approaching when, as a true servant of Michael, Francis of Assisi together with three companions, undertook what was to be a fateful destiny-laden journey to the summit of Mount La Verna, a journey during which he was to reach his life's highest fulfillment in receiving the stigmata.

With the ever-growing number of companions uniting with the order, Francis longed to find a place where he could devote himself even more intensely than hitherto, to a life of prayer and meditation; a place sufficiently remote to allow him as much freedom as possible from worldly concerns and interruptions. The ever-increasing demands made upon him because of the rapidly growing order, as well as the almost endless multitude of individuals from many places seeking his advice and longing to experience his presence—all this taken together made the requirement for such a place of seclusion ever more acute.

In May 1213 this need was met from an unexpected quarter, through the deep admiration and interest felt for Francis by a certain Count Orlando of Chiusi, whose castle of San Leo was situated at Montefeltro. On their way to Romagna, Francis and Brother Leo were passing near the village of Montefeltro, when they heard from the people that a great banquet and festival were being held at the castle to celebrate the knighting of one of the Orlando sons. Francis said to brother Leo, "Let us go up to that festival, for there with God's help we shall gather some good spiritual fruit."

In the main square of the village where all the people were assembled, Francis, moved by the Holy Spirit, preached so fervently and lovingly that everyone was profoundly moved by his words. Afterward, Count Orlando, touched to the heart through what Francis had said, took him aside and asked if he could speak to him about the salvation of his soul. Francis willingly agreed, and at the end of their conversation, Count Orlando said to him: "Brother Francis, I own a mountain in Tuscany which is very solitary and wild and is perfectly suited for someone who wishes to do penance in a place far from other people and to live a solitary life. It is called Mount La Verna. If that mountain should please you and your companions, I shall gladly give it to you for the salvation of my soul." [*The Little Flowers of St. Francis*]

Later, after Francis had returned to Santa Maria degli Angeli, he requested two of the brothers to visit the mountain. They were accompanied by fifty armed men sent by Count Orlando to protect them from wild beasts. Upon their return, they informed Francis that they were certain that this lonely mountain was most suitable as a place for solitary contemplation and prayer.

During the following years, Francis and some of his companions made repeated visits to Mount La Verna. Finally, in the summer of 1224, Francis resolved to make a longer than usual stay there, in order to celebrate the entire Michaelmas Lent in that mountain wilderness, a period of forty days of prayer and fasting extending from the festival of the assumption of the virgin (August 15) to Michaelmas Day (September 29). The observance of this Michaelmas Lent originated from Francis's profound veneration for the Archangel Michael, who as he observed, should be reverenced because "one of his principal tasks is to offer the deeds of men to God."

In his unique and incomparable biography of Francis of Assisi (1981, pp. 551–52), Arnaldo Fortini vividly describes Mount La Verna and the decisive role it was to play in the life of Francis of Assisi:

> La Verna is a mountain surmounted by an immense cliff, rising vertically, cut off from the rest of the mountain on all sides. A

thick forest covers the top. Dante described it as the *crudo sasso*—harsh crag—located between the Tiber and the Arno. It is a mass of stone crowned by furious storm clouds. A retreat for prayer in the harshness of winter. An altar in the heart of holy Italy, between its two seas, between the sources of two of its immortal rivers, whose waters have mirrored ages of iron and bronze. It was called "the great castle of the soul" by the most passionate of all the mystics, Teresa of Avila. There are no better words for it. This mountain is truly a fortress destined for terrible battles of body and soul.

In vain one searches here for the peace that Orlando had promised to Francis. The whole gigantic crag seems tormented, wounded, and broken in some horrendous convulsion. Violent passion made greivously immobile lurks in the fearsome rock that is constantly assaulted by storms, rock that seems as if from another world. In winter it lies under the icy pall of snow, in summer the stone grows scorching hot. Often it is crowned by livid lightning from beneath flying black clouds and trembles under the long rolling of thunder.

It is said that its name came from the terrible winter weather (*inverno*) experienced on its heights. Sometimes in the January nights, when the cold north wind sweeps from one peak to another, from every cliff, every abyss, every inaccessible chasm, from all the lost precipices, voices not human rise up, like shackled, unearthly spirits in frightful torment. It is said that even up here the demons did not give a moment's peace to Francis during his harrowing vigils.

This fortress does not bring to mind angelic ecstasies. It is more a setting for a battle of Titans. Covering the rocky rampart, which on all sides plunges downward in a straight line, are fearful bastions, enormous towers, inaccessible citadels, all made by the bedlam of twisted rock. According to Francis, God revealed to him that those enormous fissures and chilling precipices were made in the hour that Jesus died, when, as the Gospel records, "the rocks split." And here, where the mountain had responded to the spasm of the earth in Galilee, the wounds of the Passion were to come again in answer to a prayer, this time to Francis, the Poverello of Christ.

On his journey to Mount La Verna in August 1224, Francis took three brothers with him in order that together they might experience the Michaelmas Lent in this solitary mountain fastness. As related in the Gospel of St. Matthew, chapter 17, when Jesus ascended the Mountain of the Transfiguration, he was accompanied by three of his disciples, James, the man of wisdom ("If any of you lack wisdom, let him ask of God and it shall be given him." Epistle of James 1:5), John, whose writings teach that above all "God is love" (1 John 4:16), and Peter, the man of choleric, impetuous deeds (John 18:10). In similar manner, three companions were chosen by Francis to accompany him to the summit of Mount La Verna: Brother Masseo of Marignano, originally from Assisi, a man of profound thought, great learning, and eloquence; the second was one of Francis's closest companions, a man of simplicity, of deep warmth and purity of heart. This was Brother Leo, to whom Francis often confided his most intimate aspirations and experiences. Brother Angelo Tancredi of Rieti was his third companion. Of noble birth, he was a man of valorous action, the first knight who had joined the Order of the Friars Minor.

At dawn on the third day of their travels it became necessary to ask a peasant to lend them his donkey, since Francis, because of exhaustion and lack of sleep, was too weak to continue on foot. Upon hearing that the donkey was needed for Francis of Assisi, the good man, with great care and devotion, saddled the animal, helped Francis mount it, and accompanied the brothers on their way as the path began to lead steeply upward toward the summit. From this point *The Little Flowers of St. Francis* continues the story with touching simplicity:

> When they had climbed about halfway up the mountain, because the summer heat was very great and the path was long and steep, the peasant began to suffer intensely from thirst. He called to Saint Francis: "I am dying of thirst. If I don't have something to drink, I'll suffocate in a minute!" Saint Francis immediately got off the donkey and began to pray. He remained kneeling on the ground, lifting his hands toward heaven, until he knew by revelation that God had granted his prayer. Then he said to the peasant: "Run quickly to that rock, and there you will find running water which Christ in his mercy has just caused to flow from the rock." The man ran to the place which Saint Francis had shown him, and found a very fine spring that had been made to flow through the hard rock by the power of Saint Francis's prayer. The peasant drank all he wished, and felt better. It truly seems that the spring was

produced by a divine miracle through the prayers of Saint Francis, because neither before nor afterward was any spring to be found there or anywhere nearby. After he had done this, Saint Francis, with his companions and the peasant, gave thanks to God for having shown them this miracle. And then they traveled on.

When at last they reached the summit of Mount La Verna, a great flock of birds of many kinds flew around them in a transport of joyous welcome, and Francis saw in this a sign that it was God's will that there on this lonely mountain summit they should pass their days in fasting and prayer in honor of the Michaelmas Lent. During their stay, a falcon which was nesting nearby became a great friend of Francis's in spite of the fact that such birds are usually hostile and unwilling to associate with men. In the middle of each night, the falcon woke Francis with its song just at the time he was to rise to say the office. However, when Francis was at times exhausted from prayer and fasting, the falcon took pity on him and did not wake him so early, as if he had been instructed to permit the man of God to rest a little longer. On such days, he would call him with his bell-like song, just as daylight was appearing.

It was before dawn of the day of the Exaltation of the Holy Cross (September 14) that Francis, kneeling outside the entrance to his hermit's cell, turned his face toward the east and prayed with pronounced fervor, as recorded in *The Little Flowers of St. Francis*:

> My Lord Jesus Christ, I pray you to grant me two graces before I die: the first is that during my life I may bear in my soul and in my body, as much as possible, that pain which you sustained in the hour of your most bitter passion. The second is that I may feel in my heart, as much as possible, that excessive love with which you, O Son of God, were enflamed in willingly enduring such suffering for us sinners. After remaining for a long time in that prayer, he understood that God would grant it to him and that it would soon be conceded to him to feel those things as much as is possible for a mere creature.

His prayer was answered. The spiritual path, which began with his embrace of the leper on the road near the hospital of San Lazzaro, had found its direction in the significant words spoken from the crucifix at

11. Francis receiving the stigmata. Miniature from a manuscript of *The Golden Legend*, Jacobus de Voragine, ca. 1300. *(Henry E. Huntington Library, San Marino, California.)*

San Damiano, had rejoiced exceedingly in the courage and devotion of Saint Clare and her sisters, and in the foundation of their Order of the Poor Clares, had experienced the horrors, sufferings, and defeat at Damietta, now reached its apotheosis in this supreme moment on Mount La Verna. Suddenly it was as though the mountain burst into flame, light blazing everywhere. Far below in the valley, shepherds tending their flocks were gripped by fear, believing that the mountain was being consumed by fire, while at a still greater distance drovers, awakened by the intense light, and thinking that day was breaking, stirred their sleeping animals and set out on their way. Meanwhile on the mountain itself, as *The Little Flowers of St. Francis* recounts: "While Francis was thus inflamed in this contemplation, he saw coming down from heaven a seraph with six resplendent and flaming wings. As the seraph, flying swiftly, came closer to Saint Francis, so that he could perceive him clearly, he noticed that he had the likeness of a crucified man, and his wings were so disposed that two wings extended above his head, two were spread out to fly, and the other two covered his entire body. Upon beholding this, Saint Francis was very much afraid, and at the same time he was filled with joy and grief and amazement. He felt intense joy from the friendly look of Christ, who appeared to him in a very familiar way and gazed at him very benignly. But on the other hand, seeing him nailed to the cross, he felt boundless grief and compassion. Finally he was greatly amazed at such an astounding and extraordinary vision, for he knew well that the affliction of suffering is not in accord with the immortality of an angelic seraph. And while he was marveling thus, he who was appearing to him revealed to him that this vision was shown to him by divine providence in this particular form, in order that Francis should understand that he was to be utterly transformed into the direct likeness of the Christ crucified, not by physical martyrdom, but by the enkindling of the mind.

During that seraphic apparition, Christ, who appeared to Saint Francis, told him certain secret and profound things which the saint was never willing to reveal to anyone while he was alive, but after his death he revealed them in these words: "Do you know what I have done?" asked Christ. "I have given you the stigmata which are the emblems of my passion, so that you may be my standard-bearer. And as I descended into limbo on the day when I died and took from there by virtue of these stigmata of mine all the souls I found there, so I grant to you that every year on the day of your death you may go to purgatory and by virtue of your stigmata, you may take from there and lead to paradise all the souls of your three orders, that is the Friars Minor, the Sisters (Poor Clares), and the Continent (Third Order), and also others who have been very devoted to you, whom you may find there, so that you may be conformed to me in death as you are in life."

The account in *The Little Flowers of Saint Francis* continues:

> Now when, after a long time and a secret conversation, this wonderful vision disappeared, it left a most intense ardor and flame of divine love in the heart of Saint Francis, and it left a marvelous image and imprint of the Passion of Christ in his flesh. Soon there began to appear in the hands and feet of Saint Francis the marks

of nails such as he had just seen in the body of Jesus crucified, who had appeared to him in the form of a seraph. Likewise, in his right side appeared the wound of a spear thrust, which was open, red, and bloody, and from which blood often issued from the holy body of Saint Francis and stained his habit. And although he tried hard to hide and conceal from them these glorious stigmata, which had thus been clearly imprinted in his flesh, on the other hand he saw that he could scarcely hide them from his intimate companions. . . .

Now although those very holy wounds, inasmuch as they were imprinted on him by Christ, gave him very great joy in his heart, nevertheless they gave unbearable pain to his flesh and physical senses. Consequently, being forced by necessity, he chose Brother Leo, who was simpler and purer than the others, and he revealed everything to him, and he let him see and touch those holy wounds. Saint Francis entrusted his wounds only to him to be touched and rebound with new bandages. . . . Sometimes it happened that when Brother Leo was changing the bandage of the wound in the side, Saint Francis, because of the pain which he felt from the loosening of the bloody bandage, would put his hand on Brother Leo's chest over his heart. And from the contact of those holy hands on which were imprinted the venerable stigmata, Brother Leo would feel such sweetness and devotion in his heart that he nearly fainted and fell to the ground.

Shortly before his death, Francis's warmth of heart and deep love for Brother Leo found tender expression in the prayer he wrote especially for him:

> God bless you and keep you.
> May God smile on you, and be merciful to you;
> May God turn his regard toward you
> and give you peace.
> May God bless you, Brother Leo.

Through these simple words, uttered by one heart speaking to another, we can begin to sense something of the grandeur and majesty of Francis of Assisi, as the one who was able through divine grace to so enlarge his heart that it embraced not only his entire being, but all creatures of the earth, as well as the souls of all who came into contact with him.

12.
Francis returning from Mount La Verna. Drawing by E. Burnand. (*Facchinetti, San Francesco d'Assisi, p. 440.*)

13.
Letter to Brother Leo in the handwriting of Francis.

❧ 6 ❧

The Birth of the Canticle of the Creatures— Il Cantico delle Creature

Accompanied by Brother Leo, Francis left Mount La Verna on the day after Michaelmas 1224 in a state of agonizing suffering and near blindness. Upon reaching Assisi, he settled in a little hut made of rushes which had been built for him by the brothers at his request, located outside the cloister of San Damiano. For some time the latter had become the home of the Poor Clares, and here Santa Chiara, their spiritual leader, was destined to live as the head of their order for twenty-seven years after Francis's death.

Here Francis found himself also living near the home of the aged priest, who so long ago had taken him in as a young man who was about to have the miraculous experience of hearing the voice of the Lord speaking to him from the crucifix in the half-ruined chapel. Francis's modest rush hut was set in a peaceful location, protected from the sharp winds, and on clear afternoons it was bathed in the last rays of the setting sun.

In this humble surrounding, although racked by severe suffering and despite the outer darkness, cold and snow of the winter months, Francis experienced the acme of his life's striving, entirely permeated as it was by love. It was then that he truly recognized everything in God's creation as his brothers and sisters. In the midst of pain and privation, he had at last attained the highest goal he had set before himself: to be at one with the entire created world and all its creatures. For him at this moment, the whole universe was transfigured through his spiritual vision, despite physical blindness, weakness, and bodily agony.

As Thomas of Celano recalled:

> One night when Francis was exhausted more than usual because of his severe infirmities, he nevertheless kept the shield of patience

unshaken by praying to Christ. Finally as he prayed in agony, the lord gave him this promise of eternal life. "If the whole bulk of the earth and the whole universe were made of precious gold without price, and it was given to you as a reward for these severe sufferings which you are enduring, and instead you would be given a treasure of such great glory, in comparison with which that gold would be as nothing, not even worthy of mention, would you not be happy and would you not willingly bear what you are bearing?" "I would indeed be happy," Francis replied, "and I would rejoice beyond all measure." "Rejoice!," the Lord exclaimed, "for your sickness is a promise of my kingdom. Therefore await your inheritance of that kingdom, steadfast and assured, because of the merit of your patience."

In great exultation, blessed as he was by such a glorious promise, Francis rejoiced, and with almost superhuman patience and love he embraced the sufferings of his body. Although at that moment he was not at once able to give full expression to everything he felt, it was soon after this that he composed *The Canticle of Brother Sun,* later to be called *The Canticle of the Creatures.*

However, the spiritual joy that filled his entire being as a result of this unparalled revelation was clouded, nonetheless, by his awareness that human beings everywhere were misusing the creatures that had been given to them freely by God. Shortly afterward Francis said to his brothers: "For his praise, I wish to compose a new hymn about the Lord's creatures, whom we use daily, without whom it is impossible for us to live, and yet in misusing them we greatly offend our Creator."

Arnaldo Fortini described the true essence of Francis's motivation in writing *The Canticle of Brother Sun* in these words: "It is not only the human being who sings praises to God. His is but one song in a chorus of all creatures. God is best praised when all the songs are joined together and all creation sings in unison." And the poem in which Francis expressed these thoughts in words, with his consummate skill as a poet and as a true servant of the Lord, was described by Thomas of Celano as: "A song of cornfields and vineyards, stones and forests and all the beautiful things of the fields, fountains of water and the green plants of the gardens, earth and fire, air and wind, to love God and serve Him willingly. Finally, he called all creatures Brother, and in a most extraordinary manner, a manner never experienced by others, he discerned the hidden things of nature with his sensitive heart, as one who had already entered into *the freedom of the glory of the sons of God."* (Romans 8:21).

The Canticle of Brother Sun

Most High, all powerful, all good, Lord!
    All praise is yours, all glory, all honor
    And all blessing.

To you alone, Most High, do they belong.
    No mortal lips are worthy
    To pronounce your name.

All praise be yours, my Lord, through all that you have made,
    And first my lord Brother Sun,
    Who brings the day; and the light you give to us through him.

How beautiful is he, how radiant in all his splendor!
    Of you, Most High, he bears the likeness.

All praise be yours, my Lord, through Sister Moon and Stars.
    In the heavens you have made them,
    Bright and precious and fair.

All praise be yours, my Lord, through Brothers Wind and Air,
    And fair and stormy, all the weather's moods,
    By which you cherish all that you have made.

All praise be yours, my Lord, through Sister Water,
    So useful, lowly, precious and pure.

All praise be yours, my Lord, through Brother Fire,
    Through whom you brighten up the night.
    How beautiful is he, how gay! Full of power and strength.

All praise be yours, my Lord, though Sister Earth, our mother,
    Who feeds us in her sovereignty and produces
    Various fruits with colored flowers and herbs.

At this exalted moment, Francis was filled with a quiet satisfaction, a sense of gratitude in having created this joyful hymn embracing Brother Sun, Sister Moon and Stars, Brothers Wind and Air, Sister Water, Brother Fire, Sister Earth—a poem which expressed the truth he had long been seeking. The three lines concerning Sister Earth were followed by these final lines of summation: "Praise and bless my Lord, and give him thanks, / And serve him with great humility."

In addition to this, Francis composed a melody to go with the words of his poem, and sent some of the brothers to various places in order that in singing it they would convey its profound truth to their listeners. He instructed them in how to do this: like traveling medieval minstrels who sang of brave knights and their true loves, they were to form a circle in marketplaces and town squares, wherever people gathered. One of their number was to preach a sermon, and immediately afterward all of them were to sing Francis's *Canticle of Brother Sun*. The one who had preached was then to turn to the people and say, "We are the wandering minstrels of God and the only reward we ask is that you lead a life of true penitence."

In response to the brothers' surprise at thus being called "itinerant minstrels," Francis asked: "Who indeed are God's servants, if not minstrels who seek to move men's hearts in order to lead them into the joys of the spirit?" From this time onward, despite his steadily increasing weakness and suffering, for Francis it was sufficient to hear his Brothers sing his "canticle of joy," in order that he himself could find the courage and strength to bear every burden laid upon him.

•   •   •

In July 1225, as the result of a dispute between Podestà Oportulo and the representatives of the pope, Bishop Guido of Assisi excommunicated the podestà. (This was the same Bishop Guido who had interceded between the then youthful Francis and his father, Pietro Bernardone, many years earlier.) In response, the podestà decided on reprisals, forbidding any further economic dealings between the citizens of Assisi and the bishop and his followers. These actions, like a fire in dry tinder, speedily resulted in violent deeds of hatred and revenge between the two opposing factions.

Meanwhile, the reports of these events caused great sadness in Francis and the brothers, particularly since both the bishop and the podestà had long been among the most devoted supporters of their order. Motivated by Christ's teaching: "Blessed are the peacemakers, for they shall be called the children of God," knowing that discord and hatred can only be overcome by a spirit of true forgiveness, harmony, and love, Francis added the following lines to his *Canticle of Brother Sun*:

> All praise be yours, my Lord, through those who grant pardon
>> For love of you; through those who endure
>> Sickness and trial.

> Happy those who endure in peace,
>> By you, Most High, they will be crowned.

In the medieval *Legend of Perugia* details of what followed are recorded:

> Francis then called one of his companions and said to him: "Go and find the podestà and tell him for me that he should go to the bishop's palace with the notables of the *comune* and with all those he can assemble." When the brother had left, he said to the others: "Go, and in the presence of the bishop, of the podestà, and the entire gathering, sing the Canticle of Brother Sun. I have confidence that the Lord will put humility and peace in their hearts, and that they will return to their former friendship and affection."
>
> When everyone had gathered in the forecourt of the bishop's palace, the two brothers stood up, and one of them was the spokesman: "Despite his sufferings, blessed Francis," he said, has composed "Praises of the lord for all his creatures, to the praise of God and for the edification of his neighbor. He therefore asks you to listen with great devotion."
>
> With that they began to sing. The podestà stood up and joined his hands as for the gospel of the Lord, and he listened with great recollection and attention. Soon tears flowed from his eyes, for he had great confidence in blessed Francis and devotion for him. At the end of the canticle, the podestà cried out before the entire gathering: "In truth I say to you, not only do I forgive the lord bishop whom I ought to recognize as my master, but I would even pardon my brother's and my own son's murderer!" He then threw himself at the feet of the bishop and said to him: "For the love of our Lord Jesus Christ and blessed Francis, his servant, I am ready to make any atonement you wish!" The bishop stood up and said

to him, "My office demands humility of me, but by nature I am quick to anger; you must forgive me!" With great tenderness and affection, both locked arms and embraced each other.

The brothers were in admiration to see that the sanctity of blessed Francis had fulfilled to the letter what he had said of the peace and concord which thus would be restored between the two men. All who witnessed the scene ascribed the grace so promptly given to the two adversaries as a miracle due to the merits of the saint. These two men, forgetting all past offensive words and after such a great confrontation, returned to a very great concord.

At that moment, it seemed to all those who were gathered there in the forecourt of the bishop's palace, that the peace of the very archangels themselves had descended into the hearts of the men who had found their way to grant pardon to each other.

•   •   •

At Michaelmas 1226, it became clear to those around him that the twilight hours of Francis's life were fast approaching. In the gathering shadows as he drew near the threshold of death, despite all agony, weakness and indescribable suffering, Francis often broke into rapturous song. In these moments his heart was filled with great joy and thanksgiving, as the heavenly, angelic world began to open before him:

> Most high, all-powerful, all good Lord!
> All praise is yours, all glory, all honor
> And all blessing.

And when he no longer had strength to continue, he often asked the brothers who were with him to take up the singing of this melody of praise.

It was at this time that Dr. Bongiovanni Buono, a physician and old friend from Arezzo, came to visit Francis, and the latter asked: "What do you think about my condition?" The doctor replied: "Brother, God willing, all will be well with you." But Francis persisted, saying: "Tell me the truth. What is your real opinion? Because, by the grace and help of the Holy Spirit, I am so united with my Lord that I am equally content to live or die." The physician then answered him with directness: "According to our medical knowledge, your disease is incurable and I believe you will die either at the end of September or in early

14. Francis's farewell blessing to Assisi. Woodcut by Fritz Kunz. (*Facchinetti, San Francesco d'Assisi*, p. 465.)

October." Then Francis, most reverently and devoutly stretching out his hands to God, said, "Welcome, Sister Death! Indeed, if it be my lord's pleasure that I shall die soon, call Brothers Angelo and Leo and let them sing to me." And when they had come to him, although filled with sorrow and grief, they sang *The Canticle of Brother Sun*, which Francis had composed. However, before they reached the final verse, Francis stopped them and added these lines of praise addressed to Sister Death:

> All praise be yours, my Lord, through Sister Death,
>> From whose embrace no mortal can escape.
>> Woe to those who die in mortal sin!
>
> Happy those she finds doing your will!
>> The second death can do no harm to them.
>
> Praise and bless my Lord, and give him thanks,
>> And serve him with great humility.

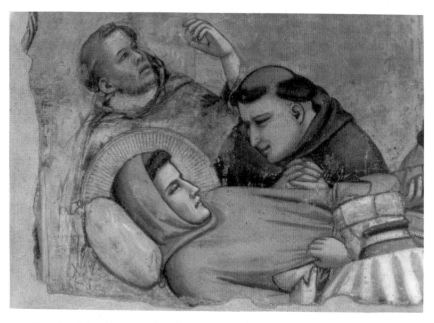

15. Death of St. Francis (detail). Fresco by Giotto, the Bardi Chapel, Sta. Croce, Florence. (*Casa Editrice Giusti di Becocci, Florence.*)

The physician's prediction was fulfilled, when only a few days afterward, late on Saturday evening, October 3, 1226, Francis crossed the threshold of death at the Porziuncola in Santa Maria degli Angeli. Although the darkness of night had already fallen, the arrival of Sister Death was accompanied by the jubilant singing of a great flock of larks in the trees surrounding Francis's hut, reminding those present of how often and lovingly he had preached to these humble, feathered creatures of the fields and forest. Further, according to an old Assisi tradition, the bells in the little church of San Stefano far away within the walls of Assisi, began to ring without the aid of human hands, their solemn tones rising like a prayer into the wooded slopes of Mount Subasio.

These signs and many others clearly reveal that at that very moment the traditionally dreaded Angel of Death had been transformed into Francis's Sister Death, bringing him an assurance of heavenly mercy, comfort and joy.

. . .

The Canticle of the Creatures

Most High, all powerful, all good, Lord!
    All praise is yours, all glory, all honor
    And all blessing.

To you alone, Most High, do they belong.
    No mortal lips are worthy
    To pronounce your name.

All praise be yours, my Lord, through all that you have made,
    And first my lord Brother Sun,
    Who brings the day; and light you give to us through him.

How beautiful is he, how radiant in all his splendor!
    Of you, Most High, he bears the likeness.

All praise be yours, my Lord, through Sisters Moon and Stars,
    In the heavens you have made them,
    Bright and precious and fair.

All praise be yours, my Lord, through Brothers Wind and Air
    All fair and stormy, all the weather's moods,
    By which you cherish all that you have made.

All praise be yours, my Lord, through Sister Water,
    So useful, lowly, precious and pure.

All praise be yours, my Lord, through Brother Fire,
    Through whom you brighten up the night.
    How beautiful is he, how gay! Full of power and strength.

All praise be yours, my Lord, though Sister Earth, our mother,
    Who feeds us in her sovereignty and produces
    Various fruit with colored flowers and herbs.

All praise be yours, my Lord, through those who grant pardon
    For Love of you; through those who endure
    Sickness and trial.

Happy those who endure in peace,
    By you, Most High, they will be crowned.

All praise be yours, my Lord, through Sister Death,
    From whose embrace no mortal can escape.

Woe to those who die in mortal sin!
    Happy those She finds doing your will!
    The second death can do no harm to them.

Praise and bless my Lord, and give him thanks,
    And serve him with great humility.

Il Cantico delle Creature

Altissimo, onnipotente bon Signore,
    tue so le laude, la glória, e l'onore
    e onne benedizione.

Ad te solo, Altissimo, se confano
    e nullo homo ene digno te mentovare.

Laudato sie, mi Signore, cum tette le tue creature,
    spetialmente messer lo frate Sole
    lo quale iorna et allumini noi per loi.

Et ellu è bello e radiante sun grande splendore:
    de te, Altissimo, porta significatione.

Laudato si, mi Signore, per sora luna e le stelle:
    in celu l'ai formate clarite e pretiose e belle.

Laudato si, mi Signore, per frate Vento
    e per Aere e nubilo e sereno et onne tempo,
    per lo quale a le tue creature dai sustentamento.

Laudato si, mi Signore, per sor Acqua,
la quale è molto utile et humile e pretiosa e casta.

Laudato si, mi Signore, per frate Focu,
per lo quale enn'allumini la nocte.
Et ello è bello ocundo e robustoso e forte.

Laudato si, mi Signore, per sora nostra matre Terra,
la quale ne sustenta e governa
e produce diversi fructi con coloriti fiori et herba.

Laudato si, mi Signore, per quelli che perdonano per lo tuo amore
e sostengono infirmitate e tribulatione.

Beati quelli che 'l sosterranno in pace,
ca da te, Altissimo, sirano incoronati.

Laudato si, mi Signore, per sora nostra Morte corporale,
da la quale nullo omo vivente po' scampare.

Guai a quelli che morrano ne la peccata mortali!
Beati quelli che trovarà ne le tue santissime voluntati,
ca la morte seconda non li farrà male.

Laudate e benedicete mi Signore
e rengratiate e serviteli cun grande humilitate.

＊ 7 ＊

The World of the
Celestial Hierarchies

Francis of Assisi recognized that behind all the phenomena of nature, beings of the spiritual world, the celestial hierarchies are at work. This becomes obvious in the light of Francis's words of poetic power and directness of purpose which he included in his Rule of 1221:

> Almighty God . . . with your own holy will you created all things physical and spiritual; we beg all the choirs of the blessed spirits, seraphim, cherubim, thrones, dominions, powers, mights, principalities; we beg all the choirs of archangels and angels, . . . we beg them all most humbly, for love of you, to give thanks to you, the most high, eternal God, living and true, with your son, our beloved Lord Jesus Christ, and the Holy Spirit, the comforter, for ever and ever. Amen. [chapter 23: "Prayer, praise, and thanksgiving"]

From this, one can rightly conclude that Francis was entirely aware of the existence of the celestial hierarchies as described in a work attributed to Dionysius the Areopagite. The latter was long thought to have been one of the Athenians who listened to St. Paul preach on Mars Hill, as related in Acts 17. His manuscript entitled *The Celestial Hierarchies* was traditionally believed to have been sent by the Byzantine Emperor Michael the Stammerer to Louis the Pious of France about the year A.D. 827. Subsequently the Greek manuscript was entrusted to the famous Johannes Scotius Erigena (800–877), the Celtic monk, philosopher, and theologian of the ninth century, who was the first to translate it into Latin at the request of Charles the Bald of

France, son of Charlemagne. This appears to have been the only Latin translation until the twelfth century (the time of Francis of Assisi), when two others were also made. Although factual details about the author, date, and place of writing of The Celestial Hierarchies are unknown, nevertheless the fifteenth chapter of this book exerted a tremendous influence among scholars and theologians throughout the whole of the Middle Ages and long after.

In the west, traces of this book may be found in the writings of many of the scholastic authors—for example, Albertus Magnus and Thomas Aquinas. In literature, we find its influence in the works of Latini, Dante, Spencer, and Milton. It formed the canon of angelic lore for the painting, sculpture, and mosaics of the Middle Ages.

The general principle of *The Celestial Hierarchies* concerns the transmission of life from God "downward," through descending orders of mediating beings to humanity. Between this source that is the triune God, and man, the celestial hierarchies are ranged in three triads: seraphim, cherubim, and thrones; dominions, virtues, and powers; principalities, archangels, and angels. Their collective activity is to lift humanity to God through purification, illumination, and perfection. Dionysius indicates that the "highest" triad, nearest to God, contemplates the divine intelligence and reflects it onward to the second triad, while the third triad ministers to humanity directly. The sources of these names are to be found in the Old Testament, in later Jewish writings, and in the epistles of Saint Paul (Eph. 1:21 and Col. 1:16).

·   ·   ·

In the third part of his *Divine Comedy*, the *Paradiso*, Tenth Canto, Dante Alighieri (1265–1321) places Dionysius the Areopagite among the theologians in the heaven of the sun:

> Nearby behold the lustre of that taper,
> > Which in the flesh below looked most within
> > The angelic nature and its ministry.

Later in the *Paradiso*, Dante describes in detail the Intelligenze Celesti (the name by which the nine hierarchies were known to the scholastics of the later Middle Ages, including Thomas Aquinas) through the following words of Beatrice in the Twenty-eighth Canto:

And she, who saw the dubious mediations
    Within my mind, "the primal circles," said,
    "Have shown thee Seraphim and Cherubim,
Thus rapidly they follow their own bonds,
    To be as like the point as most they can,
    And can as far as they are high in vision.
Those other Loves, that round about them go,
    Thrones of the countenance divine are called,
    Because they terminate the primal Triad.
And Thou shouldst know that they all have delight
    As much as their own vision penetrates
    The Truth, in which all intellect finds rest.
From this it may be seen how blessedness
    Is founded in the faculty which sees
    And not in that which loves, and follow next;
And of this seeing merit is the measure,
    Which is brough forth by grace, and by good will;
    Thus on from grade to grade doth it proceed.
The second Triad, which is germinating
    In such wise in this sempiternal spring,
    That no nocturnal Aries despoils,
Perpetually hosanna warbles forth
    With threefold melody, that sounds in three
    Orders of joy, with which it is intrined.
The three Divine are in this hierarchy,
    First the Dominions, and the Virtues next;
    And the third order is that of the Powers.
Then in the dances twain penultimate
    The Principalities and Archangels wheel;
    The last is wholly of Angelic sports.
These orders upward all of them are gazing,
    And downward so prevail, that unto God
    They all attracted are and all attract
And Dionysius with so great desire
    To contemplate these Orders set himself,
    He named them and distinguished them as I do."
                      —*Longfellow, trans. (1867)*

In his scholarly notes to his translation of Dante's *Divine Comedy*,
Henry Wadsworth Longfellow (1807–1882) commented on the nature

of the "divine intelligences" mentioned in the Second Canto of the *Paradiso* as follows:

> The Intelligences, ruling and guiding the several heavens, receiving power from above and distributing it downwards, taking their impression from God and stamping it like a seal upon the spheres below, according to Dionysius the Areopagite, are:

	Seraphim	Primum Mobile
Godhead	Cherubim	Fixed Stars
	Thrones	Saturn
	Dominions	Jupiter
Christ	Virtues	Mars
	Powers	Sun
	Principalities	Venus
Holy Spirit	Archangels	Mercury
	Angels	Moon

In his copious notes to the Twenty-eighth Canto of the *Paradiso*, a part of which is quoted above, Longfellow had provided extensive information concerning the relationship between *The Celestial Hierarchies* of Dionysius and the commentary on this work in the *Summa Theologica* (chap. 50–64 and chap. 106–114) of Thomas Aquinas (1227–1274). In what follows, it will be noted that Thomas Aquinas often quotes Dionysius, in certain instances even giving his exact words, but more often amplifying and interpreting Dionysius's meaning:

> The name of seraphim is not given from love alone, but from excess of love, which the name of heat or burning implies. Hence Dionysius interprets the name *Seraphim* according to the properties of fire, in which is excess of heat. In fire, however, we may consider three things. First a certain motion which is upward and which is continuous; by which is signified, that they are unchangingly moving towards God. Secondly, its active power, which is heat. . . . and by this is signified the influence of this kind of Angels, which they exercise powerfully on those beneath them, exciting them to

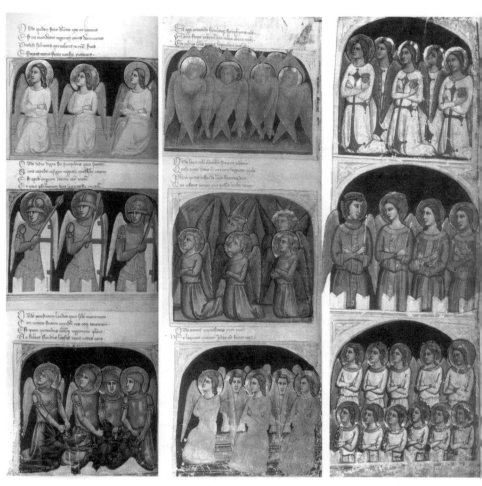

16. The nine celestial hierarchies. From a fourteenth-century Italian manuscript. (*British Library, Board Headquarters, 96 Euston Road, London NW11 2DB, England.*)

a sublime fervor, and thoroughly purifying them by burning. Thirdly, in fire its brightness must be considered; and this signifies that such Angels have within themselves an inextinguishable light, and that they perfectly illuminate others.

In the same way the name of the cherubim is given from a certain excess of knowledge; hence is it interpreted *plenitudo scientiae*, which Dionysius explains in four ways: first, as perfect vision of God; secondly, full reception of divine light; thirdly, that in God himself they contemplate the beauty of the order of things emanating from God; fourthly, that, being themselves full of this kind of knowledge, they copiously pour it out upon others.

The order of the thrones excels the inferior orders in this, that it has the power of perceiving immediately in God the reasons of the Divine operations. . . . Dionysius explains the name of the thrones from their resemblance to material chairs, in which four things are to be considered. First, in reference to position, because chairs are raised above the ground; and thus these angels, which are called Thrones, are raised so far that they can perceive immediately in God the reasons of things. Secondly, in material chairs firmness much be considered, because one sits firmly in them, but this is *e converso,* for the angels themselves are made firm by God. Thirdly, because the chair receives the sitter, and he can be carried in it; and thus the angels receive God in themselves, and in a certain sense carry him to their inferiors. Fourthly, from their shape, because the chair is open on one side, to receive the sitter; and thus these angels, by their promptitude, are open to receive God and to serve him.

And thus Dionysius, from the name of the orders inferring the properties thereof, placed in the first hierarchy those orders whose names were given them in reference to God, namely the seraphim, cherubim, and thrones; but in the middle hierarchy he placed those whose names designate a certain common government or disposition, that is, the dominions, virtues, and powers; and in the third hierarchy he placed those whose names designate the execution of the work, namely the principalities, angels, and archangels. But to the rule of government three things belong, the first of which is the distinction of the things to be done which is the province of the dominions; the second is to provide the faculty of fulfilling, which belongs to the virtues; but the third is to arrange in what way the things prescribed, or defined, can be fulfilled, so that someone may execute them, and this belongs to the powers. But the execution of the angelic ministry consists in announcing things divine. In the execution, however, of an act, there are some who begin the act, and lead the others, as in singing the precentors, and in battle those who lead and direct the rest; and this belongs to the principalities. There are others who simply execute, and this is the part of the angels. Others hold an intermediate position, which belongs to the archangels.

As noted above, one of the sources frequently referred to in the manuscript of *The Celestial Hierarchies* by Dionysius the Areopagite was the writing of the prophets of Old Testament times. A further parallel can be drawn between the mystical writings of the early Hebrew kabbalists involving the spiritual nature and the creative activity of each letter of the Hebrew alphabet. According to these ancient teachings, the entire visible world and all the phenomena of nature therein, derived from the words spoken by God, since "in the beginning God created the heavens and the earth." (Let there be light; Let the dry land appear; etc.) Therefore, the esoteric meaning of each letter was considered to be a contributing element in the divine creation.

In the kabbalistic tradition, the beings of the universe are divided into three *provinces:* 1. The Angelic World or the several orders of angels or pure celestial beings in heaven. 2. The Starry World. 3. The Elemental World.

The nine Hebrew letters from Aleph to Jod inclusive can be regarded as descriptive of each of the nine orders of angels in turn. According to the kabbalists, the activity of these beings of the nine celestial orders derives from the power of God, and flows downward step by step from the highest—the seraphim—to the lowest—the angels, whose influence reaches further below, culminating in the creation beneath them.

Hence, a relationship undoubtedly exists between the mystical essence of each of the first nine letters of the Hebrew alphabet and the nine manifestations of nature as invoked by Francis of Assisi in his *Canticle of the Creatures.* This will be further developed in chapter 8 following.

* * *

In the centuries following the death of Francis of Assisi, his world of chivalry and knighthood, of pious hermit and wandering minstrel, of religious pilgrimage and miracle play, so characteristic of the medieval time, gave way to the new learning, the humanism, the centralized governments, the scientific investigation, the expanding horizons, both physical and mental, of the Renaissance. No single part of human life was untouched by the change. In the political, religious, social, intellectual spheres, the Renaissance worked its wonders, and the dream of the Middle Ages awakened to the glorious colors of the dawn of a new world—our modern world.

The transformation in human beings included a break with their former way of looking at the earth beneath their feet, at their fellow men, and at the blue vault arching over their heads. From a conception of nature that saw the animate in everything, even in stones—new systems of classification, ways of analysis, of explanation, based more and more upon the evidence of the physical senses, and less and less upon folklore and tradition—came into being. The new cosmopolitanism, the recovery of the art and philosophy of ancient Greece, the breaking up of old parties and practices in the social and political life led ultimately to man's growing consciousness of *himself,* and of his intrinsic worth as a being among other beings. The discovery of the shape of the earth, the rebirth of geographic learning lost in the dimness of forgotten ages, finally brought men to think of the possiblity of worlds beyond this world, of whole solar systems beyond ours, and the word *infinite* began to assume a new importance. In the genius of language is revealed the momentous change that took place in these centuries. One need only recall that to the medieval mind the word *reality* referred exclusively to spiritual, heavenly things, to see how far-reaching was the change that occurred at the dawn of our modern world.

Following the Renaissance came the age of the baroque, in which yet further unfoldments in human consciousness, in science and the arts, occurred. One of the many notable achievements of the baroque was in the development of the art of music. In this, Johann Sebastian Bach (1685–1750) played a dominant creative role and left an indelible mark on the entire history of musicology from his time to our own.

Johann Wolfgang von Goethe (1749–1832), "the sage of Weimar," master of poetry, prose, drama, and natural science, in recalling the fortnight visit which the young composer-conductor Felix Mendelssohn (1809–1847) made to the Goethe house in the Frauenplan at Weimar in 1830, later exclaimed: "When I heard Mendelssohn playing Bach's music for me, it seemed as though in it I heard God at work creating the world."

This remarkable statement is a kind of "bridge" between Francis of Assisi's inspired expression of his love, gratitude and joy for all God's creations, and Goethe's perception of the divine at work as he experienced it through the medium of the music of Bach. This mighty creative power attained one of its most notable heights in Bach's well-known *Goldberg Variations,* completed in 1742. Often referred to as "The Aria with Thirty Variations," it was composed for one of Bach's former students, Johann Theophilus Goldberg to play for his patron, the Baron von Keyserling, who frequently suffered long, sleepless nights and periods of deep melancholy. Lying in his bed, the baron never tired of hearing Goldberg play these variations on the harpsichord in an adjoining room.

Through these thirty variations, Bach also spoke to the learned musicians of his day, giving them not only a unique set of lessons in baroque counterpoint, but at the same time illustrating a profound spiritual reality in the series of nine canons, which serve to separate each successive pair of variations. It is in the progression of these nine canons that Bach's incomparable spiritual insight and technical facility leads the listener on an ascending musical path through the nine stages of creation.

This ascending path stands in contrast to the descending path in the unfolding of the celestial hierarchies, the beings of the spiritual world which, as has been shown, are undoubtedly related to the manifestations of nature represented by Francis of Assisi in his *Canticle of the Creatures.*

A careful examination of the successive intervals employed in Bach's composition of these canons reveals that they are presented in a well-defined ascending order as though through them Bach wished to lead the baron from the latter's everyday earthly concerns, stage by stage, into the highest realms of the spiritual world—that is, from the realm of the angels to the heights of the seraphim.

In the music of the age of Romanticism, a similar ascending path of spiritual unfoldment can be experienced in the order of the nine symphonies of Beethoven (1770–1825), culminating in the triumphant, Seraphic *Ode to Joy,* which forms the closing movement of the Ninth Symphony.

*   *   *

During the first quarter of our present century, Rudolf Steiner, in his books and lectures, described in great detail remarkable ideas and insights regarding the nature and working of the beings of the spiritual hierarchies. These ideas originated from his own deep insight and penetration into the knowledge of the world of nature and spirit, expressed by him in terms suited to our modern consciousness. Rudolf Steiner's contribution to this area of spiritual-scientific knowledge and its relation to Dionysius the Areopagite and the Old and New Testaments, can be more clearly grasped by means of the following outline:

	The Bible	Greek	Dionysius	Rudolf Steiner
First *Hierarchy* *(Father God)*	Seraphim Cherubim Thrones	Seraphim Cherubim Thrones	Seraphim Cherubim Thrones	Spirits of Love Spirits of Harmony Spirits of Will
Second *Hierarchy* *(Christ)*	Dominions Powers or Virtues Mights	Kyriotites Dynamis Exusiai	Lordships Powers Authorities	Spirits of Wisdom Spirits of Motion Spirits of Form
Third *Hierarchy* *(Holy Spirit)*	Principalities Archangels Angels	Archai Archangeloi Angeloi	Principalities Archangels Angels	Spirits of Personality Spirits of Fire Spirits of Twilight

In a lecture given in Helsinki in 1912, Rudolf Steiner observed that: "all the forces and activities proceeding from the successive orders of the beings of the spiritual hierarchies, are made visible in the collective phenomena of earthly man and nature." Later he wrote in an essay concerning the Archangel Michael: "one must more and more lay aside the view of an indefinite spiritual existence (some pantheistic sea of causation existing at the foundation of all things), and must pass on to a more definite and concrete view that rises to conceptions of the distinct *spiritual beings* of the higher hierarchies."

It was through the inspiration of these *spiritual beings* that Francis was enabled to set forth the ninefold path as he revealed it for us in his *Canticle of the Creatures*, thus leading the individual human being to the experience of the oneness of divine creation.

The Canticle of the Creatures: A Living Organism

From his boyhood Francis of Assisi had always been drawn to poetry and music through the folk songs and verses he had heard from his mother in his childhood years. This attraction was further deepened by his youthful participation in the festivities of the Tripudianti. The background to this were the popular lyrics and songs of the famous troubadours of the time, as well as his interest in knightly ideals, all of which were a part of his cultural heritage. Francis was also gifted with a splendid singing voice and a sensitive ear for music and verse, embracing the inherent color-qualities of words. All of these gifts remained alive within him to the end of his life.

Like a skilled and gifted painter, he used the light, life, and color of language to move men's hearts and minds. The ultimate expression of his creative love of poetry reached its climax in the lines of *The Canticle of the Creatures*, written in the dialect of the Umbrian people. This work is generally considered to be the earliest example of lyric poetry in the Italian Language—and is said to be the true historical source of Western nature poetry.

This achievement alone would have been sufficient to ensure Francis of Assisi a lasting place in the history of Italian literature. Nevertheless, of far greater importance is the fact that, in addition to its qualities as an outstanding creative work of poetry, *The Canticle of the Creatures* is clearly the genuine outpouring of a heart immersed in deepest prayer and contemplation. The joy expressed in it is all the more extraordinary if one realizes that it was composed during his last illness when his body was racked with intense suffering. Yet the Canticle itself expresses no hint of anything except deepest gratitude, reverent joy, and limitless love. It is a true hymn of thanksgiving!

In the text of the Italian original, the word *per* (through) is repeated frequently, but is often overlooked by translators of the canticle into the English language, when in a number of instances the word *for* is used instead of *through*. This, however, alters a most fundamental point which Francis wished to express in the canticle—namely, that all creation is the means through which God himself is "praised and glorified"—not that God is to be praised and thanked *for* all things created by him. Therefore not only the sun, moon, stars, and the four elements, but even forgiveness, suffering, and death are shown to be the means by which the creator is "honored and blessed."

In his silent contemplation of the beauties of nature during his solitary walks through the fields of the valley below Assisi ("I have seen nothing lovelier than my Valley of Spoleto"—Francis of Assisi) and in the Umbrian forests on the slopes of Mount Subasio, Francis' heart opened again and again to behold all that surrounded him in the sky above, the creations of nature around him, and the ground beneath his feet. In all this he experienced the tones of a true symphony of gratitude and praise to God, the creator of all.

Thus it was abundantly clear to Francis that the whole of nature is the means *through* which God is eternally being glorified.

*   *   *

In *The Canticle of the Creatures*, consisting to begin with of seven invocations, and endearingly called the "Canticle of Brother Sun" by Francis, one catches a glimpse of the medieval system of education through the Seven Liberal Arts. These were first set forth by Martianus Capella, an African grammarian of the fifth century and author of the famous work on the seven arts, regarded at that time as the single, outstanding treatise on this subject. This system was further amplified in the Middle Ages by Alanus ab Insulis, John of Salisbury, Bernardus Silvestris, and other well-known teachers of the School of Chartres.

These seven liberal arts were divided into two groups, the trivium consisting of three foundational subjects: grammar, rhetoric, and dialectic. These in turn were followed by the quadrivium comprising the four subjects pertaining to the higher grades of education: arithmetic, geometry, music, and astronomy. This system formed the fundamental basis of all educational training during the Middle Ages, including the time of Francis of Assisi, Dante and later the scholastics. Secular education was given in conjunction with theological training as well, and consisted precisely in the cultivation and development of the trivium and quadrivium.

From most ancient times, the power of human speech was regarded as the principal bridge between humankind and the entire universe, as expressed archetypically in the words of Genesis: "And God said. . . ." Therefore, when the man of antiquity spoke, he felt instinctively that in the alphabet, as in one great primordial sentence, he was voicing the entire glory of the divine being. Already in prehistoric eras, man experienced a reverential relationship between his speech and astronomical realities and truths.

In early ages and onward into historical times, it was so that to be versed in grammar signified that a man had become aquainted with the true mysteries of the single letters of the alphabet. In each of these he learned to know the star related to it. Rhetoric implied that he could apply and put into practice the astronomical lore he had made living within him. Dialectic was the process of grasping and elaborating this substance in thought, in the idea.

Arithmetic was known to embrace the mysteries of numbers. Rudolf Steiner indicated that in this connection the unit was always taken as the starting point, as the greatest and most all-embracing element. The unit separated and the two arose, similarly the three, and so on. Today, as the outcome of our atomistic thinking, we regard this process from the opposite point of view—that is, we take the unit as the smallest and arrive at the two and the three by addition. The ancient way, however, led onward from the primal unit organically into the reality of the mysteries of number. So too in geometry—until the feeling arose that geometry, truly conceived, is the "music of the spheres." Geometrical forms were eventually experienced as musicals tones. From geometry one passed upward to music, and finally to astronomy as the highest of the seven arts, returning, now with full consciousness, to the point of departure, to the idea fully realized.

The three Liberal Arts of the trivium (Grammar, Rhetoric, Dialectic) were considered to be spiritual or supernatural in nature—just as in his Canticle Francis placed Sun, Moon and Stars as the first three "Creatures" though whom God is to be praised. From another point of view, these may be characterized in the words of St. Paul as "Faith, Hope and Charity." (Cor. 1, Chapter 13)

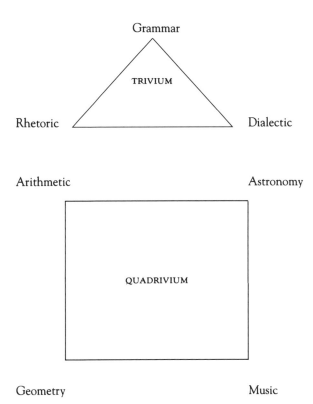

On the other hand, the four higher subjects of the quadrivium (Arithmetic, Geometry, Music, Astronomy) were considered to express the four Cardinal Virtues, i.e., prudence, justice, temperance, and fortitude. In his canticle, Francis referred to these as the four elements, wind and air, water, fire, earth.

The artistic portrayal of the Seven Liberal Arts which most faithfully follows the imagery of the "seven maidens" described by Martianus Capella, is to be found carved in stone on the Royal Portal of the cathedral of Chartres, dating from the twelfth century. We see them there just as he describes them, and at the base of each is represented a personage of distinction in the corresponding science—for example, Aristotle, Pythagoras, Euclid, and Ptolemy.

*   *   *

Thus *The Canticle of the Creatures* as originally written by Francis of Assisi can be seen as an expression of the medieval preoccupation with *order*, as the first characteristic of the creative process. This enthusiasm for order was linked to an equal appreciation of *symmetry*, which the medievalist considered to be the prerequisite of a kind of intuitive *inner harmony*. This inner harmony, particularly in literature, was the fruit of the unquestioned recognition of the power inherent in numbers, originating with the Greeks, and continuing into the earliest times of Christianity. The power of number found classic expression in the words of St. Augustine, Bishop of Hippo (A.D. 354–430), who called them "thoughts of God." He continued: "The divine wisdom (Sophia) is reflected in the numbers which are imprinted on all things. Therefore, the physical and spiritual worlds are united and based upon the eternal quality of numbers." In his view as well as in that of the scholars of the Middle Ages, beauty is a harmonious accord and the science of numbers is the science of the universe which reveals its secrets through numbers. Therefore, as Francis of Assisi well knew, the one who can enter into the inner mysteries of numbers finds in them the divine architectural plan forming the bridge from the latter to the archetypal created world of nature.

In the original form of *The Canticle of the Creatures*, one finds first of all the number three, predominately the symbol of the divine trinity, the trivium, expressed in the personifications of Brother Sun, Sister Moon, and Sister Stars. This is already epitomized in the words of Genesis 1:16: "And God made two great lights; the greater light to rule the day and the lesser light to rule the night; he made the stars also." A similar use of the trivium, the threefoldness of the divine, is to be found in Dante's *Divine Comedy*, which is like an edifice constructed entirely of numbers, fundamentally based on the figure three. This is clearly to be seen in the three sections of the work: the *Inferno*, *Purgatorio*, and *Paradiso*, as well as in the basic form of the verses, the *terzarima*, as Dante composed them.

The second section of the canticle as originally composed by Francis of Assisi appears as a fourfold organism, the quadrivium, finding expression as a kind of realization or reflection of the basic source-idea of the trivium. Here the earthly elements play a leading role in contrast to that of the sun, moon, and stars in the opening section of the canticle. The four elements express the four states of being manifested in the material world: gaseous, liquid, heat, or warmth, and solid, and find personification in Brothers Wind and Air, Sister Water, Brother Fire, and Sister Earth.

As one penetrates into the order and symmetry of the liberal arts, one can see them reflected in Francis's creativity, expressed in the architecture of this extraordinary work *The Canticle of the Creatures:*

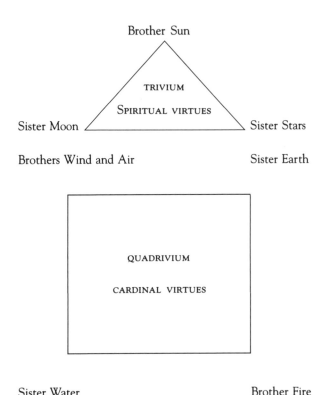

In chapter 6 it has been pointed out that after the completion of the sevenfold "Canticle of Brother Sun," some months later Francis added the invocation addressed to those who "grant pardon," as well as those who "endure sickness and trial." Finally as Francis neared the threshold of death, the concluding lines of the canticle were written, calling upon Sister Death as an instrument in praising the lord.

These two additional sections complete the nine-fold structure of Francis's *Canticle of the Creatures*, widening its scope to include all humankind and their earthly destinies, because the meeting with Sister Death is an experience which occurs only at the conclusion of one's path of earthly life.

A careful study of the canticle in its final form as Francis bequeathed it to us shows that the central body of the work is framed by an introduction of six lines and is concluded by two final lines of praise. In the body of the poem, Sister Moon and Stars, though grouped together in a single line, are clearly to be regarded as two different manifestations in the heavens. On the other hand, reflection will show that the twin Brothers Wind and Air, are in reality two aspects of one and the same element, and therefore form a oneness. Near the end of the canticle, those who "grant pardon" and those who "suffer" are actually an expression on Francis's part in response to a single historical event as already described in chapter 6.

Therefore, as a ninefold organism, *The Canticle of the Creatures* includes all humanity in a harmonious oneness, together with the original sevenfold representation of all creation, both earthly and heavenly. From ancient times onward, the figure nine has been widely considered as representing the completion of a cycle, a symbol of immutable truth, an image of perfection and of the absolute. Nine contain the unique mathematical property of ever reproducing itself—that is, twice $9 = 18$, $1 + 8 = 9$; $3 \times 9 = 27$, $2 + 7 = 9$: $4 \times 9 = 36$, $3 + 6 = 9$, and so on. Something of this is expressed in the fact that nine is the result of the multiplication of the trinity by itself, thus achieving the absoluteness of the absolute.

In Dante's *Divine Comedy*, as has been shown, the figure three forms the archetypal basis of the artistic structure and essence of the work. In Francis's *Canticle of the Creatures* one can see that this threefold principle has been lifted to a new dimension in which the ninefold arrangement now portrays the existence of universe, earth and humanity in a fully objective, artistic manner.

In the light of all of the foregoing, Francis's canticle can speak to us as a unique ninefold path consisting of nine stages leading to inner enlightenment, a meditative way suited to the consiousness and capacities of people of our time who are in search of a reliable means to genuine spiritual experience. Indeed, the canticle can become an instrument by which today we may find a satisfying and profound relationship with the world of nature, humanity, and the divine.

It is this recognition of the almost endless possibilities arising from such a penetration into the inner nature of the canticle which has led to the preparing of the nine sections of the following chapter of this book. While this insight may appear to be new to some readers, in reality, as a potenial, it has been expressed in various ways by writers and artists throughout the centuries. One example of this ninefold path is clearly revealed in the highly descriptive lines by John Milton (1608–1674):

> Ring out, ye crystal spheres
> Once bless our human ears,
> If ye have power to touch our senses so;
> And let your silver chime
> Move in melodious time;
> Letting the deep bass of Heaven's organ blow;
> Thus, with your ninefold harmony,
> Make up full consort to the angelic symphony.

17. St. Francis and the seraph. Line drawing from a thirteenth-century marble sculpture, Chapel of the Stigmata at Mount La Verna. *(Casa di Preghiera, Santuario Francescano, 52010 La Verna.)*

9

The Ninefold Path
of the Canticle Today

This chapter is based upon the nine sections of *The Canticle of the Creatures*, arranged so as to illustrate each successive petition in the following five ways:

First   The quotation of the lines from the canticle in relation to Francis of Assisi himself.

Second   The related passage from *The Celestial Hierarchies* by Dionyisus the Areopagite.

Third   Commentary from the ancient Hebrew kabbala, together with passages from the Old and New Testaments.

Fourth   Selected extracts from Rudolf Steiner's writings and lectures.

Fifth   In conclusion, a collecteanea of illustrative examples from literature.

· 1 ·

About Brother Sun—The Seraphim

For Francis of Assisi, the seraphim, in their love and glory are expressed in the sun itself, as the first among all creation named in his *Canticle of the Creatures*:

All praise be yours, my Lord, through all that you have made,
　　And first my lord Brother Sun,
　　Who brings the day; and light you give to us through him.

How beautiful is he, how radiant in all his splendor!
　　Of you, Most High, he bears the likeness.

The words of King David, "O Lord, I love the beauty of thy house," found ardent expression in the being of Francis of Assisi. Hand in hand there walked within his heart, his love for poverty and for beauty as well. For him, the "house" of which the psalmist sang included the entire majestic sweep of creation, from the lowliest worm to the highest spiritual beings in the heavens. To Francis, beauty was the manifestation of the glory of all creation on the earth in the fullest sense—manifested in the household of God—in the heavens, in men and in the love of God himself. Just as Dante beheld at the height of his heavenly journey "the love that moves the sun and other stars," for Francis this love was the primal evidence of the loftiest rank in the angelic world—the seraphim—as described by Dionysius the Areopagite in his *Celestial Hierarchies:*

> The name *Seraphim* clearly indicates their heat and keenness, the exuberance of their intense perpetual tireless activity, and their energetic assimilation of those below themselves, kindling and firing them to their own heat, and entirely purifying them by a burning and all-consuming flame; and by their unhidden, unquenchable, changeless, radiant, and enlightening power, dispelling and destroying the shadows of darkness.

Because of their fiery nature as described above by Dionysius, the seraphim were visually depicted from most ancient times as clothed in the color red. In sculptured form they appear, for example, in the porch of Chartres Cathedral carrying flames and balls of fire.

* * *

"And God said, let there be lights in the firmament of the heaven to divide the day from the night. And God made . . . the greater light to rule the day." —Genesis 1:14,16

"Above the throne stood the seraphim: each one had six wings; with twain he covered his face, and with twain he covered his feet, and with twain he did fly." —Isaiah 6:2

א ALEPH, the first letter of the Hebrew alphabet. The kabbalists identify this as the Holy Name hu, expressive of the inaccessible light (shekinah) of the divine being. Aleph is generally referred to as the *en soph*, the infinite, the most sublime and perfect crown (kether) of creation (Stehelin, *Rabbinical Literature*, vol. 1).

·   ·   ·

The sublime beings of the first order of the celestial hierarchies are traditionally called seraphim or "spirits of love." In lectures given in Dusseldorf, Germany, in 1909 entitled "The Spiritual Hierarchies," Rudolf Steiner said: "The name *Seraphim*, rightly understood in the sense of ancient Hebrew esotericism, is always interpreted as referring to beings who received the loftiest ideas and aims of a cosmic system from the trinity. The seraphim, cherubim, and thrones are beings who are closest to the Godhead. In Western Christian esoteric thought, they are appropriately described as enjoying the unveiled countenance of the Godhead."

·   ·   ·

In his famous collection of poems, gathered from the Gaelic of the Scottish Hebrides, titled *Carmina Gadelica*, Alexander Carmichael (1832-1912) included the two following selections, expressing with remarkable simplicity the essence of the words by Francis of Assisi regarding Brother Sun:

The Sun

The eye of the great God,
The eye of the God of glory,
The eye of the King of hosts,
The eye of the King of the living
Pouring upon us
At each time and season,
Pouring upon us
Gently and generously.

Glory to thee,
Thou glorious sun.

Glory to thee, thou sun,
Face of the God of life.

Easter Sunday

The people say that the sun dances on this day in joy for a risen Savior. Old Barbara Macphie at Dreimsdale saw this once, but only once, during her long life. And the good woman, of high natural intelligence, described in poetic language and with religious fervor what she saw or believed she saw from the summit of Benmore:

> The glorious gold-bright sun was after rising in the crests of the great hills, and it was changing color—green, purple, red, blood-red, white, intense-white and gold-white, like the glory of the God of the elements to the children of men. It was dancing up and down in exaltation at the joyous resurrection of the beloved savior of victory.
>
> To be thus privileged, a person must ascend to the top of the highest hill before sunrise, and believe that the God who makes the small blade of grass to grow is the same God who makes the large, massive sun to move.

· 2 ·

About "Sister Moon"—The Cherubim

All praise by yours, my lord, through Sister Moon.

Francis of Assisi loved Sister Moon, silent and white, particularly as she arose from behind the massif of Mount Subasio, casting mysterious shadows through the dense pine forests, her rays magically illuminating the details of villages and towns, houses and fields in the lovely valley of Spoleto. Through the heavenly artistry of Sister Moon, the entire landscape was blended into a hymn like that of the cherubim, the spirits of harmony, in the ancient eastern liturgy: "Glory to the holy life-creating, undivided mystery of the trinity, now and evermore, unto ages of ages."

The magical beauty of the working of Sister Moon is further enhanced and amplified through the following words of Dionysius the Areopagite in his *Celestial Hierarchies:*

> The name *Cherubim* means "fullness of knowledge." Through them the providential energy streams forth as a transcendental light perfectly illuminating the soul, uniting it with the divine wisdom, and imparting a full and lucid understanding of the divine immanence in all things.
>
> The name *Cherubim* denotes their power of knowing and beholding God, their receptivity to the highest gift of light, their contemplation of the beauty of the godhead in its first manifestation, and that they are filled by participation in divine wisdom, and bounteously outpour to those below them from their own fount of wisdom.

*   *   *

BETH (house), The second letter of the Hebrew alphabet: indicates the wisdom of God, the source of all lesser beings. In the kabbala it is called *hochmah*, that is, wisdom. This is connected with the order of spiritual beings called ophanim, that is, wheels, forming the second order of the cherubim. (Stehelin, *Rabbinical Literature,* vol. 1.)

Rudolf Steiner often refers to the cherubim as the "spirits of harmony," and in his lectures entitled "The Spiritual Hierarchies" he continues:

> The cherubim have the task of elaborating in wisdom the aims and ideas received from the divine. The cherubim are thus spirits of exalted wisdom, capable of transposing into workable plans what is indicated by the seraphim. . . . Our forefathers, through tradition, represented the cherubim as strangely winged beasts with variously shaped heads: the winged lion, the winged eagle, the winged bull, and the winged man. For the cherubim, in fact to begin with, drew near to man from four sides. They approached in shapes that could afterward be represented and thus become known as the form of the cherubim. The latter were subsequently given the names bull,

lion, eagle, and man, which in Christian esotericism were adapted in picture form as designations for each of the writers of the four gospels: Matthew, angel/man; Mark, lion; Luke, bull; and John, eagle. . . . The seraphim, cherubim and thrones are the beings who are closest to the Godhead. In Western Christian esoteric thought they are appropriately described as "enjoying the unveiled countenance of the Godhead."

*   *   *

Hymn of the Cherubim
from the liturgy of Saint John Chrysostom,
of the Eastern Orthodox Church

We who mystically image the cherubim,
Who sing to the life-giving trinity
The thrice-holy hymn,
Let us now lay aside all earthly cares

For now we are to receive the king of all,
Invisibly escorted by the ranks of angels,
Alleluia, Alleluia, Alleluia!

Johann Wolfgang von Goethe wrote the following about Sister Moon in his drama, *Faust 1*:

O full moon, I so oft
At midnight watched you climb aloft—
I would on mountain heights
With you go onward in your lovely light!

In nineteenth-century American poetry, Longfellow (*Evangeline*, Book 1) composed the following lines concerning Sister Moon:

Serenely they saw the moon pass
Forth from the folds of a cloud,
And one star follow her footsteps,
As out of Abraham's tent
Young Ishmael wandered with Hagar.

Finally, Alexander Carmichael included this prayer in his collection of
Scottish Hebridian verse:

The New Moon

She of my love is the new moon,
The King of all creatures blessing her;
Be mine a good purpose
Towards each creature of creation.

Holy be each thing
Which she illumines;
Kindly be each deed
Which she reveals.

Be her guidance on land
With all beset ones;
Be her guidance on the sea
With all distressed ones.

May the moon of moons
Be coming through thick clouds
On me and on every mortal
Who is coming through affliction.

May the virgin of my love
Be coming through dense dark clouds
To me and to each one
Who is in tribulation.

May the King of grace
Be helping my hand
Now and forever
Till my resurrection day.

•   •   •

· 3 ·

About Sister Stars—The Thrones

All praise by yours, my Lord though sister. . . stars,
In the heavens you have made them,
Bright and precious and fair.

As Arnaldo Fortini once so beautifully described, "Francis loved the
virgin stars, whose brightness alternately burns and dims as they twin-
kle, light and dark all through the night. In solitude and in silence
they shine, creatures that bring to mind Saint Clare and her sisters at
San Damiano, whose chaste beauty was burning hidden in their sanctu-
ary among the olive trees, solely for the praise of God."

In a harmonious echo of Francis of Assisi's words about the stars as
his third invocation, the description of the thrones as the third hierarchical order of spiritual beings in the words of Dionysius the Areopagite echoes:

> The thrones make manifest the purifying power of providence
> which wholly penetrates the consciousness. Through them the soul
> is uplifted to the divine and becomes established in the constancy
> of divine service.
> The name of the most glorious and exalted thrones denotes that
> which is exempt from and untainted by any base and earthly thing.
> For these have no part in that which is lowest, but dwell in fullest
> power, immovable and perfectly established in the Most High, and
> receive the divine immanence above all passion and matter, and
> manifest God, being attentively open to divine participations.

* * *

GIMEL (restoring or rewarding), the third letter of the Hebrew
alphabet, denotes the holy name Asch, signifying the Holy Spirit.
It is often referred to as Binah—that is, Prudence or Arahim, great,
valiant angels of might. These form the third order of spiritual beings,
flowing from the divine source, and illuminated by the power of God.
They, together with the seraphim and cherubim, form the first and
highest hierarchy of the celestial world (Stehelin, *Rabbinical Literature*,
vol. 1).

Rudolf Steiner frequently referred to the thrones as the spirits of will, and continues his description of the first hierarchy thus: "The thrones have the task, figuratively speaking, of putting into practice the lofty cosmic thoughts that have been conceived in wisdom, thoughts received by the seraphim from the divine, and pondered over by the cherubim. . . . The thrones appear to us as beings endowed with the power to transpose into a primary reality what has been first conceived by the cherubim. . . . Thus the seraphim, cherubim, and thrones are the beings who are closest to the Godhead. In Western Christian eso-teric thought they are appropriately described as "enjoying the unveiled countenance of the Godhead."

*   *   *

Look, how the floor of heaven
Is thick inlaid with patines of bright gold;
There's not the smallest orb which thou behold'st,
But in his motion like an angel sings,
Still quiring to the young-eyed cherubims;
Such harmony is in immortal souls!
—William Shakespeare (1564–1616),
The Merchant of Venice

Star of descending night! fair is thy light in the west! Thou liftest thy unshorn head from thy cloud; thy steps are stately on thy hill. What dost thou behold in the plain? The stormy winds are laid. The murmur of the torrent comes from afar. Roaring waves climb the distant rock. The flies of evening are on their feeble wings; the hum of their course is on the field. What dost thou behold, fair light? But thou dost smile and depart. The waves come with joy around thee; they bathe thy lovely hair. Farewell, thou silent beam! Let the light of Ossian's soul arise!

The above lines from James Mcpherson's edition of *The Poems of Ossian* (1762), were greatly appreciated by Goethe and were translated by him into German.

Silently, one by one, in the infinite meadows of heaven,
Blossomed the lovely stars, the forget-me-nots of the angels.
—Longfellow, *Evangeline*, Book 1

Song of the Stars

Look, look, through our glittering ranks afar,
In the infinite azure, star after star,
How they brighten and bloom as they swiftly pass!
How the verdure runs o'er each rolling mass!
And the path of the gentle winds is seen,
Where the small waves dance, and the young woods lean.

And see, where the brighter day-beams pour,
How the rainbows hang in the sunny shower;
And the morn and eve, with their pomp of hues,
Shift o'er the bright planets and shed their dews;
And twixt them both, o'er the teeming ground
With her shadowy cone the night goes round!

In the above lines by one of the well-known poets of nineteenth-century New England, William Cullen Bryant (1794-1878), as in the other passages quoted above, the mood of Francis of Assisi's *Sister Stars* is poetically echoed. This is also true of the following poem, by one of America's best-loved nineteenth-century poets:

When I Heard the Learn'd Astronomer

When I heard the learn'd astronomer,
When the proofs, the figures were arranged in columns
    before me,
When I was shown the charts and diagrams, to add, divide,
    and measure them,
When I sitting heard the astronomer where he lectured
With much applause in the lecture room,
How soon unaccountable I became tired and sick,
Till rising and gliding out I wander'd off by myself,
In the mystical moist night-air, and from time to time,
Look'd up in perfect silence at the stars.
                    —Walt Whitman (1819–1892)

· 4 ·

About Brothers Wind and Air
—The Dominions (Kyriotetes)

All praise by yours my Lord, through Brothers Wind and Air,
    And fair and stormy, all the weather's moods,
    By which you cherish all that you have made.

With this invocation Francis opens the next section of his *Canticle of the Creatures*, devoted to the four elements. The first element is the airy or gaseous state, of which he says: "Fair and stormy, all the weather's moods." This latter characterization expresses, though in a somewhat different form, the thoughts of Dionysius the Areopagite regarding the dominions or Kyriotetes:

> The second triad, the dominions, virtues, and powers, are given the middle place as indicating the ordered governance of providence. Through them the soul is liberated from all that is below and assimilated to that which is above (see outline in chapter 7 above). The dominions impart order and justice through which true liberty is gained. The name given to the holy dominions signifies a certain unbounded elevation to that which is above, freedom from all that is of the earth, and from all inward inclination to the bondage of discord, a liberal superiority to harsh tyranny, an exemptness from degrading servility and from all that is low; for they are untouched by any inconsistency. They are true lords, perpetually aspiring to true lordship, and to the source of lordship, and they providentially fashion themselves and those below them, as far as possible, into the likeness of true lordship. They do not turn towards vain shadows, but wholly give themselves to that true authority, forever one with the Godlike source of Lordship.

*   *   *

DALETH (a gate), the fourth letter of the Hebrew alphabet, denotes the holy name *El*, and is referred to as *chesed*—that is, grace or mercy. This refers to the angelic order of spiritual beings known as dominions, or in Greek, Kyriotetes (Stehelin, *Rabbinical Literature*, vol. 1).

Rudolf Steiner frequently uses the name "spirits of wisdom" for these spiritual beings, the dominions, who stand highest in the middle triad of the nine celestial hierarchies. In his lectures "The Spiritual Hierarchies" he says the following about the beings of the second triad:

> In descending to the next hierarchy, to the beings called dominions, powers, and mights, or spirits of wisdom, movement and form, we find that they do not have such an immediate view of the Godhead. They no longer behold God in his immediate form, they behold his manifestation, as he reveals himself, if I might put it so, through his countenance. For them it is unmistakably the Godhead, and they too have the immediate impulse to carry out the manifestations of the Godhead as was the case for the seraphim, cherubim, and thrones. The impulse is not quite so powerful but it is, nevertheless, still an immediate one. It would be impossible for the seraphim, cherubim, and thrones not to accomplish what they behold as ordained by the Godhead; that would be unthinkable because of their proximity to the Godhead. But it would be equally out of the question for the dominions, powers, and mights to undertake something that was not willed by the Godhead himself.

*　　*　　*

The Wind

Who has seen the wind?
Neither you nor I,
But when the trees lift up their heads,
The wind is passing by.
— William Blake (1757–1827)

O wild West Wind, thou breath of Autumn's being,
Thou, from whose unseen presence the leaves dead
Are driven, like ghosts from an enchanter fleeing,
Yellow and black, and pale, and hectic red,
Pestilence-stricken multitudes: O thou
Who chariotest to their dark wintry bed
The wingèd seed, where they lie cold and low,
Each like a corpse within its grave, until

Thine azure sister of the spring shall blow
Her clarion o'er the dreaming earth, and fill
(Driving sweet buds like flocks to feed in air)
With living hues and odours plain and hill:
Wild Spirit, which are moving everywhere;
Destroyer and Preserver; Hear, O hear!
> —P. B. Shelley (1792–1822),
> "Ode to the West Wind"

'Twas one of the charméd days
When the genius of God doth flow;
The wind may alter twenty ways,
A tempest cannot blow.
It may blow north, it still is warm;
Or south, it still is clear;
Or east, it smells like a clover-farm;
Or west, no thunder fear.
> —Ralph Waldo Emerson (1803–1882),
> "Woodnotes"

Unwarmed by any sunset light,
The gray day darkened into night,
A night made hoary with the swarm
And whirl-dance of the blinding storm,
As zigzag wavering to and fro
Crossed and recrossed the wingéd snow.
> —John Greenleaf Whittier (1807–1892),
> the Quaker poet, in his "Snow-Bound"

Emily Dickinson (1830-1886), one of the most perceptive of the New England poets, revealed her insight into the working of the world of the elements in the following lines about Brother Wind:

The Wind

How lonesome the Wind must feel
      Nights—
When people have put out the Lights

And everything that has an Inn
Closes the shutter and goes in.

How pompous the Wind must feel
    Noons—
Stepping to incorporeal Tunes
Correcting errors of the sky
And clarifying scenery.

How mighty the Wind must feel Morns—
Encamping on a thousand dawns
Espousing each and spurning all
Then soaring to his Temple Tall.

· 5 ·

About Sister Water—The Powers (Virtues or Dynamis)

All praise be yours my Lord, through Sister Water,
    So useful, lowly, precious and pure.

In Francis's invocation to Sister Water, a new enhanced note of joyfulness resounds in the canticle, reflected in the four adjectives he uses: useful, lowly, precious, and pure. In this personification of water, one recalls the moment when, in answer to the peasant's dire need, through the power of prayer, Francis of Assisi called forth the flowing water from the rock beside the path leading to the heights of Mount La Verna. When later his life forces were ebbing away, he experienced as a living memory the days he had spent in mediation and prayer on the shores of Lake Trasimeno near Perugia, and how, when on his solitary walks, his reading of the words of the office were accompanied by the cheerful sound of the rushing water of the flowing streams. Vividly he recalled the many hours he had passed, musing upon spiritual realities while sitting beside quiet pools in which were reflected the white masses of cloud forms gently floating in the blue summer sky high above him.

This calm peaceful spirit which Francis associated with Sister Water in his canticle by no means excluded his awareness of the power and majesty of the working of the Holy Spirit. As Francis well knew, it lies behind all visible manifestations of the creator. Centuries earlier, this had been powerfully expressed by Dionysius the Areopagite in the following words concerning the virtues (powers, dynamis):

> The name of the holy virtues signifies a certain powerful and un-shakable virility welling forth into all their Godlike energies; not being weak and feeble for any reception of the divine illuminations granted to it; mounting upward in fullness of power to an assimila-tion with God; never falling away from the divine life through its own weakness, but ascending unwaveringly to the superessential virtue which is the source of virtue; fashioning itself as far as it may, in virtue; perfectly tuned toward the source of virtue, and flowing forth providentially to those below it, abundantly filling them with virtue. The virtues are the bestowers of grace and valor.

* * *

ה *HE* (behold), the fifth letter of the Hebrew alphabet, denotes the name *Pashad*—that is, severity, judgment, awe. This order of spiritual beings is referred to as *Gnaz* (strength) flowing out of the power of God (Stehelin, *Rabbinical Literature*).

Rudolf Steiner often referred to the powers as spirits of motion. They stand in the middle of the second triad of the nine celestial hierarchies, and though they no longer behold the godhead in his immediate form, they behold his manifestation as he reveals himself, and thus they too have the direct impulse to carry out the manifestations of the godhead as was the case of the seraphim, cherubim, and thrones (see the refer-ence quoted above in the section "About Brothers Wind and Air," from Steiner's "The Spiritual Hierarchies").

* * *

The Brook

I come from haunts of coot and hern,
I make a sudden sally,
And sparkly out among the fern,
To bicker down a valley.

By thirty hills I hurry down,
Or slip between the ridges,

By twenty thorps, a little town,
And half a hundred bridges.

I chatter over stony ways,
In little sharps and trebles,
I bubble into eddying bays,
I babble on the pebbles.

With many a curve by banks I fret
By many a field and fallow,
And many a fairy foreland set
With willow-weed and mallow.

I wind about, and in and out,
With here a blossom sailing,
And here and there a lusty trout,
And here and there a grayling,

And here and there a foamy flake
Upon me, as I travel
With many a silvery waterbreak
Above the golden gravel.

I steal by lawns and grassy plots,
I slide by hazel covers;
I move the sweet forget-me-nots
That grow for happy lovers.

I slip, I slide, I gloom, I glance,
Among my skimming swallows;
I make the netted sunbeam dance
Against my sandy shallows.

I murmer under moon and stars
In brambly wildernesses;
I linger by my shingly bars;
I loiter round my cresses.

And out again I curve and flow
To join the brimming river,
For men may come and men may go,
But I go on for ever.

—Alfred, Lord Tennyson (1809–1892)

The Voice of the Rain

And who art thou? said I to the soft-falling shower,
Which strange to tell, gave me an answer, as here translated:
I am the Poem of Earth, said the voice of the rain,
Eternal I rise impalpable out of the land and the bottomless sea,
Upward to heaven, whence, vaguely form'd, altogether changed,
    and yet the same,
I descend to lave the drouths, atomies, dust-layers of the globe,
And all that in them without me were seeds only, latent, unborn;
And forever, by day and night, I give back life to my own origin,
    and make pure and beautify it.

—Walt Whitman

· 6 ·

About "Brother Fire"—the Mights (Exusiai)

All praise by yours, my Lord, through Brother Fire,
    Through whom you brighten up the night.
    How beautiful is he, how gay! Full of power and strength.

The note of joyfulness that enters into the canticle in the invocation to Sister Water is now further enhanced in the above lines devoted to Brother Fire. Francis's early biographers recall that "above all creatures deprived of reason, he had the greatest love for the sun and the fire." With the coming of each new day, he rejoiced in the sun as it triumphantly rose over the summit of Mount Subasio, and each evening the fire burning in the hearth warmed not only his body but gladdened his heart, as its flickering light reflected into the dark corners of the room, lighting up the faces of his companions.

Francis regarded fire as something to be treasured, and therefore was always saddened by the extinguishing of the altar candles at the end of religious services. He instructed the brothers to burn wood until it was completely consumed, and not to extinguish half-burned brands by the custom of throwing them into the wind, realizing that the purifying flame must have its full effect.

Dionysius the Areopagite describes the inner nature, purpose, and power of the mights, revealed through the working of the elements, particularly of fire:

> The Mights or authorities give the providential aid which with irresistible power overcomes and redirects the forces which fetter the mind of man to the things of earth.
>
> The name of the holy mights together with the divine dominions and virtues, signifies an orderly and unconfined order in the divine receptions, and the regulation of intellectual and supermundane power which never debases its authority by tyrannical force, but is irresistibly urged onward in due order to the divine. It beneficently leads those below it, as far as possible, to the supreme power which is the source of power, which it manifests after the manner of angels in the well ordered ranks of its own authoritative power.
>
> This middle triad of the celestial intelligence, having these god-like characteristics, is purified, illuminated, and perfected in the manner already described, by the divine illuminations bestowed upon it in a secondary manner through the first hierarchical order, and is shown forth in a secondary manifestation by the middle choir.

*   *   *

VAU, the sixth letter of the Hebrew alphabet, refers to the mysteries of the holy name Elohim, and is described as Tiphereth—that is, beauty. These beings are otherwise known as mights, and together with the powers and dominions form the middle hierarchy of the celestial world (Stehelin, *Rabbinical Literature*).

These Mights (Elohim) or spirits of form are often referred to by Rudolf Steiner in various lectures, as for example in the following excerpt from his cycle on Genesis (1910):

> The seers of old said to themselves: "If we look upon the material substance around us, it speaks to us in the being of the thrones;

but it is permeated by an element of force which tries to bring it all into form, hence the name Spirits of Form. In all these names there is a hint of the reality they stand for. If we look at the tendency towards crystalline form around us, we have at a lower level a manifestation of the forces which weave and hold sway in the substance of the Spirits of Form, as the Elohim themselves. That is their field of action. They are the *smiths*, forging in their warmth element the crystalline forms of the different earths and metals, out of the formless matter of the spirits of will (thrones). They are the spirits who in their activity of warmth at the same time constitute the form-principle in existence."

Rudolf Steiner once spoke about fire in the following words: "Fire always built a bridge between the outer material world and the inner soul world that can be perceived only inwardly. Fire or warmth was central to all observation of nature; it was the gateway by means of which one penetrated from the outer to the inner. It is truly like a door in front of which one can stand. One can behold it from outside, one can open it, and one can behold it from within. That is the true place of fire among natural phenomena."

* * *

Salamander—A Being of Fire

Happy, happy glowing fire.
Dazzling bowers of soft retire!
Ever let my nourished wing,
Like a bat's, still wandering,
Nimbley fan your fiery spaces,
Spirit sole in deadly places,
In unhaunted roar and blaze,
Open eyes that never daze,
Let me see the myraid shapes
Of men and beasts and fish and apes,
Portrayed in many a fiery den
And wrought by spumy bitumen

On the deep intenser roof,
Arched every way aloof.
—John Keats (1795–1821)

Pictures in the Fire

"See yonder there—that's my friend," he said.
"The fire?," asked Nell the child.
"It has been alive as long as I have. We talk and think together. . . . It's like a book to me, and many an old story it tells me. It's music, for I should know its voice among a thousand, and there are other voices in its roar. It has its pictures too. You don't know how many strange faces and different scenes I trace in the red-hot coals. It's my memory, that fire, and shows me all my life."
—Charles Dickens (1812-1870),
The Old Curiosity Shop

· 7 ·

About Sister Earth—The Principalities (Archai)

All praise by yours, my Lord, through Sister Earth, our mother,
Who feeds us in her sovereignty and produces
Various fruits with colored flowers and herbs.

According to Saint Paul, to him even the rocks recalled Jesus, whom he compared to a rock that cracks in order to give water to the thirsty pilgrim as he crosses the desert of life (I Cor. 10:4). Francis of Assisi loved all aspects of mother earth: the rocky, rugged slopes of the Appenines, the rich earth of the Umbrian plain, the wild herbs, the flowers, the trees of every shape and kind, especially the shimmering light and shade of the olive groves. He often quoted the words of Job that symbolize the suffering of the just: "For a tree there is hope, if it be cut down, that it will sprout again" (Job 14:7). He took this saying so seriously that he instructed the brothers to the effect that no tree that had to be cut down was to be totally destroyed. Its stump should be left in such a condition that it could sprout again, thus providing a symbol of the hope of rebirth.

In the friars' garden, he asked that some space always be set aside for flowers, bearers of lovely color and fragrant scent, and also for herbs: thyme, mint, parsley, balm, who, he said "show God's love for men, and in them he gives us a sign of his grace."

In chapter 9 of *The Celestial Hierarchies* by Dionysius the Areopagite we are introduced to the third triad of celestial beings—those who stand nearest to man:

> There remains for us the reverent contemplation of that sacred triad which completes the angelic hierarchies, and is composed of the divine principalities, archangels, and angels. And first, I think, I ought to explain the meanings of their holy names.
>
> The name of the celestial principalities signifies their godlike princeliness and authoritativeness in an order which is holy and most fitting to the princely power, so that they are wholly turned toward the prince of princes, and lead others in princely fashion, and that they are formed, as far as possible, in the likeness of the source of principality, and reveal its superessential order by the good order of the princely powers. To the third triad of principalities, archangels, and angels belongs the final execution of the work of providence.
>
> The principalities exhibit divine lordship and true service. Through them the soul may turn from its attachment to worldly pursuits to the service of the divine, and ultimately become a co-worker with his ministers.

*　　*　　*

SAJIN (armeur), the seventh letter of the Hebrew alphabet, denotes the name Zeboath—that is, lord of hosts, also known as Netsach, conquering. This order of spiritual beings is known as that of principalities (Stehelin, *Rabbinical Literature*).

In chapter 2, above, it is said that the function of the spirits of personality, or Archai, as Rudolf Steiner portrays them, is to guide the successive historical epochs of time. Simultaneously, they are the bearers of what is individual in each human being, his ego or "I."

In another context, Steiner characterized the Archai yet from a different point of view:

> Rising a stage higher, we come to the beings known as the spirits of personality, or Archai. These are still loftier beings who have an even more exalted task in the total structure of the affairs of humanity. In essence, they govern the interrelationships of the whole of the human species on earth. They live in waves of time, change their configuration from age to age, and are able to take on a different spiritual body at the appointed moment. These beings are concerned with the significance and mission of a particular age of humanity.

. . .

The spiritual path to the heights of the divine involves tasks which humanity must perform *on earth*. But humanity must not follow this path solely egotistically and seflishly; otherwise its efforts will fail. It is only when human beings include an awareness of and gratitude for his or her relationship with and indebtedness to all the kingdoms of the earth: mineral, plant, and animal—through which he or she has been able "to climb to human's estate"—that his or her efforts can be crowned with success.

This thought was beautifully expressed by Christian Morgenstern (1871–1914), whose poem, "The Washing of the Feet" describes the warmth of self-sacrifice, and the spiritual insight that results from devotion:

> I thank you, dumb and silent stone,
> I bend in reverence to you;
> My life and growth as plant to you I owe.
>
> I thank you, fruitful earth and flower,
> I bow my head in reverence to you;
> You helped me rise to animal's estate.
>
> I thank you, stone and plant and beast,
> I make obeisance lowly to you all;
> 'Tis you have helped me to my human self.

So flows thanksgiving ever back and forth
In the divine Whole, manifold yet One,
Entwining all with threads of thankfulness.

Vladimir Soloviev (1853–1900), the Russian mystic and philosopher, was also a poet whose intimate connection with nature is shown
in the following lines, written in the quiet country of the beautiful
Tolstoy estate at Postynka, in May 1886:

Mother Earth

Mother Earth, to you I bow my head,
And through the veil of your perfumes
The burning of a kindred heart I feel,
The beating of a cosmic life I hear.

The noontide rays, with ardent joy,
Descend in blessing from the shining heaven;
In happy greeting to the silent light,
The flowing river sings, the forest rustles.

Again I see in sacrament revealed
Marriage of earth's soul to heaven's light
And in love's fire, all earthly pain
Like fleeting vapor, vanishes away.

At the end of the four sections of the canticle which concern the
four elements, the following poem is included here, since it summarizes
their essential nature in the light of Christ as lord of the elements, a
motif often described in Celtic literature:

St. Bride's Song

Christ! King of the elements, Hear me.
Earth, bear me,
Air, lift me,

Fire cleanse me,
Water, quicken me.

Christ! King of the elements, Hear me.
I will bear the burden of the earth with Thee.
I will lift my heart though the air to Thee.
I will cleanse my desire for love of Thee.
I will offer my life renewed to Thee.

Christ, King of the elements!
Water, fire, air and earth:
Weave within my heart this day
A cradle for Thy birth.
—Alexander Carmichael, "Carmina Gadelica"

· 8 ·

About "Those who Pardon, Those who Endure"—
The Archangels

All praise be yours, my Lord, through those who grant pardon
　　For love of you: through those who endure
　　Sickness and Trial.

Happy those who endure in peace,
　　By you, Most High, they will be crowned.

Undoubtedly, one of the reasons why Francis is so widely recognized and appreciated is due to his unfailing attitude of tolerance and long-suffering kindness toward those in need. It is almost commonplace to picture Francis as a kindly shepherd guiding the flocks and caring for the lambs, yet it is this very quality of wise guidance and tender care, as expressed in the above verse from the canticle, which confirms this image of Francis. The story of the events which evoked the adding of these lines to the canticle has already been related in chapter 6 above. However, Francis's entire life was devoted to compassion, tenderness, caring for the ill and suffering, as well as those in need of wise counsel, of which the instance cited above, occuring only a few months before his death, is but one of many similar examples.

18. Archangel Michael and his hosts. Woodcut by Albrecht Dürer. 1498. (*British Museum, Great Russell Street, London WC1B 3DG, England.*)

Francis well knew that any trace of revenge, hatred, or vindictiveness, if unchecked, works like a virulent poison, not only on the individuals directly concerned, but can spread throughout the whole surrounding, bringing about the destruction of the social setting in which it manifests itself. Beyond all other remedies, he recognized that in reality it is love and forgiveness which alone form the sovereign panacea for the social ills of humanity.

Out of tradition and his own life experience, Francis was aware that among the archangels Michael is related to the judgment of human souls and the just overcoming of evil, Gabriel to "peace among men on earth," Raphael to healing the wounds of sickness and trial, Uriel to the gift of warmth and light to Sister Earth. Something of this nature and activity of the archangels is expressed by Dionsysius the Areopagite in his *Celestial Hierarchies:*

> The archangels imprint on all things the divine seal whereby the universe is the written word of God; they impart to the soul the spiritual light through which it may learn to read this divine book, and also to know and use rightly its own faculties.
>
> The choir of the holy archangels is placed in the same threefold triad as the celestial principalities; for, as has been said, there is one hierarchy and order which includes these and the angels. But since each hierarchy has first, middle, and last ranks, the holy order of archangels, through its middle position, participates in the two extremes, being joined with the most holy principalities on the one hand, and with the holy angels on the other.

*   *   *

HETH, the eighth letter of the Hebrew alphabet, denotes a name of God: Elohe Zabaoth and Tehilim—that is, praise. This order is generally referred to as that of the archangels (Stehelin, *Rabbinical Literature*).

If my people shall humble themselves and pray,
and turn from their wicked ways, then will I hear
and *forgive* them their sins, and will heal their land.
(1 Chr. 7:14)

Forgive us our trespasses, as we forgive those who
trespass against us. (Matt. 6:12)

Blessed are the peacemakers; for they shall be
called the children of God. (Matt. 5:19)

Father, forgive them, for they know not what they do.
(Luke 23:34)

One of the ways in which Rudolf Steiner characterized the archangels or "spirits of fire" is:

> These beings are not concerned with single individuals. Their task is a more encompassing one. They bring about harmonizing influences among larger groups of human beings, among peoples, races, etc. They have the task within our earth evolution of bringing the individual soul into contact with the various folk souls. For one who is able to penetrate with spiritual knowledge into the reality of things, folk souls are quite different from what is generally understood by this term today. A certain number of people live in a particular area—in Germany, France, or Italy, for instance. Because our physical eyes can only perceive a number of human beings as so many outer physical forms, modern thinkers merely conceive of a folk soul as the abstract sum total of so many people.
>
> Only the individual human being is real for them, not the folk-soul. But for one who is able to look into the true workings of the spiritual world, a folk-soul is a reality. A fire spirit or archangel manifests itself in folk-soul. It governs the relationship between individual human beings and the whole of a people.

*   *   *

The Four Archangels

In the Name of God the Almighty
To my right Michael
And to my left Gabriel
And before me Uriel
And behind me Raphael
And over my head
The presence of God.
　　　　—Traditional Hebrew Prayer

Forgiveness

My heart was heavy, for its trust had been
Abused, its kindness answered with foul wrong;

So, turning gloomily from my fellow-men,
One summer Sabbath day I strolled among
The green mounds of the village burial-place;
Where, pondering how all human love and hate
Find one sad level; and how, soon or late,
Wronged and wrongdoer, each with meekened face,
And cold hands folded over a still heart,
Pass the green threshold of our common grave,
Whither all footsteps tend, whence none depart,
Awed for myself, and pitying my race,
Our common sorrow, like a might wave,
Swept all my pride away, and trembling I forgave!
          —John Greenleaf Whittier (1807–1892)

Prometheus

When your soul in single light will see
Falsehood and truth, goodness and evil,
And will embrace all the world in one greeting of love,
What is, and what has been,

Then will you know the joy of reconciliation,
Your thought will understand
That only in phantoms of childish notions
Live falsehood and evil.

Then will come the hour—last hour of creation—
When your light with single ray
A whole world of visions nebulous will disperse
Along with the heavy, earthly dream.

Barriers are falling, fetters melting
In the fire divine;
And the eternal morning of new life is dawning
In All, and All in One.
          —Valdimir Soloviev (1853–1900)

· 9 ·

About Sister Death—The Angels

All praise by yours, my lord, though Sister Death,
From whose embrace no mortal can escape.

Woe to those who die in mortal sin!
Happy those she finds doing your will!
The second death can do no harm to them.

Praise and bless my Lord, and give him thanks,
And serve him with great humility.

As has been described at the end of chapter 7 above, the writing of
these lines, which took place only a few days before Francis of Assisi's
death, conclude his *Canticle of the Creatures.*

The following lines by Dionsysius the Areopagite concerning the
angels, as the ninth order of the celestial hierarchies, conclude his
description of the path leading from the godhead (the divine trinity) through the ministering activity of the seraphim, cherubim,
thrones, the dominions, powers, mights, the principalities, archangels,
and angels, on behalf of man and all created nature:

> The angels minister to all men and the things of nature, purifying
> and uplifting them. The angels fill up and complete the lowest
> choir of all the hierarchies of the celestial intelligences since they
> are the last of the celestial beings possessing the angelic nature.
> And they, indeed, are more properly named angels by us than are
> those of a higher rank because their choir is more directly in contact
> with manifested and mundane things.
>
> Thus the revealing triad of the principalities, archangels, and
> angels presides one through the other over the human hierarchies
> so that their elevation and turning to God and their communion
> and union with him may be in order; and moreover, that the proces-
> sion from God, beneficiently granted to all the hierarchies, and
> visiting them all in common, may be in most holy order.

· · ·

TETH (departing or escaping), the ninth letter of the Hebrew
alphabet, also refers to Sadai, a name of God, or Musad—that

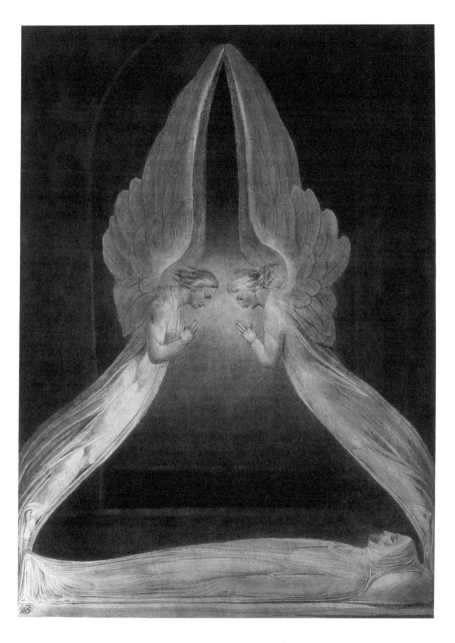

19. In the Tomb. A watercolor by William Blake (1757–1827), ca. 1806. (Victoria and Albert Museum, Cromwell Road, South Kensington, London SW7 2RL, England.)

is, ground or foundation, usually referred to as angels, or because of their connection with human birth and death, particluarly in regard to the latter, they are often called spirits of twilight (Stehelin, *Rabbinical Literature*).

When Rudolf Steiner characterizes the angels as the Sons of Twilight, this indicates their role as the "star" of the individual human being's destiny, their concern for its welfare, and above all their presence at the moment when the twilight of earthly life draws in, prior to the appearance of the light of the spiritual world breaking in upon it. As everyone acquainted with old traditions knows, each human individual has his or her own guardian angel, who stands beside him or her not only during life's course, but keeps watch at the moment of birth and guides humanity over the threshold of death.

In another context, Steiner enlarged the concept of humankind in relation to the hierarchies by characterizing man himself as "the tenth hierarchy":

> Man is a member of the hierarchies but is quite distinct from them. He is quite different from the seraphim, cherubim, thrones, the dominions, powers, mights, and also from the spirits of personality, from the archangels and from the angels. Looking into the future, he can say to himself, "I am called upon to seek the impulse for my actions in the deepest recesses of my own inner being—not by contemplating the godhead, as the serpahim do, for instance, but out of my own inner being." The Christ does not act in such a way that his impulses have necessarily to be followed; one follows him out of understanding and out of freedom. He never seeks to hinder man's free development in one or another direction. In the deepest sense of the word Christ could say, "You shall know the truth and the truth will make you free."

*   *   *

From: the Jewish Cemetery at Newport

"Blessed be God, for he created Death!"
The mourners said, "and Death is rest and peace";
Then added, in the certainty of faith,
"And giveth Life that nevermore shall cease."
                    —Henry Wadsworth Longfellow

Footsteps of Angels

When the hours of Day are
   numbered,
And the voices of the Night
Wake the better soul, that slumbered,
To a holy, calm delight;

Ere the evening lamps are lighted,
And, like phantoms grim and tall,
Shadows from the fitful firelight
Dance upon the parlor wall;

Then the forms of the departed
Enter at the open door;
The beloved, the true-hearted
Come to visit me once more.
         —Henry Wadsworth Longfellow

Because I Could Not Stop for Death

Because I could not stop for Death
He kindly stopped for me—
The Carriage held but just Ourselves—
And Immortality.

We slowly drove—he knew no haste
And I had put away
My labor and my leisure too,
For his Civility.

We passed the School where Children strove—
We passed the Fields of Gazing Grain—
We passed the Setting Sun—
Or rather—He passed Us.

We paused before a House that seemed
A Swelling of the ground—

The Roof was scarcely visible—
The Cornice—in the Ground.

Since then—'tis Centuries—and yet
Feels shorter than the Day
I first surmised the Horses' Heads
Were toward Eternity.

—Emily Dickinson

*   *   *

One of Alexander Carmichael's poems has been chosen from his Scottish Hebredian collection *Carmina Gadelica* to bring these selections concerning the nine celestial hierarchies to a close:

The Guardian Angel

Thou angel of God who hast charge of me
From the dear Father of mercifulness,
The shepherding kind of the fold of the saints
To make round about me this night;

Drive from me every temptation and danger,
Surround me on the sea of unrighteousness,
And in the narrows, crooks and straits,
Keep thou my coracle, keep it always.

Be thou a bright flame before me,
Be thou a guiding star above me,
Be thou a smooth path below me,
And be a kindly shepherd behind me,
Today, tonight, and forever.

I am tired and I a stranger,
Lead thou me to the land of angels;
For me it is time to go home,
To the court of Christ, to the peace of heaven.

Afterword

In concluding this book, we have selected the following four passages from a most perceptive contemporary work by Xavier Schnieper, *Saint Francis of Assisi* (Scala, Florence, 1981). These extracts throw light on a number of aspects of the nature and significance of Francis's life and work, which are particularly meaningful in the face of our present world situation at the end of the twentieth century.

Francis of Assisi was concerned with the fundamental destiny of man. To him this question was not an abstract one, not a theorem of philosophical or theological speculation, but in a completely modern sense, a need to find and illuminate the purpose of his own existence. These problems weighed on him explicitly as they weigh on many young people of today. Francis questioned what he could do in practical terms to liberate himself from the prescribed way of life in which human activity was not motivated by material, social, political, or religiously colored interests. He was seeking to discover how human beings can release forces enabling peace, freedom, nonviolence, and brotherliness to begin to leaven human society.

* * *

At a decisive turning-point in his life, Francis wrote with classical simplicity: *Uscii dal mondo* (I renounced the world). The literal translation of this phrase may be misleading. In the language of Francis and the *Fioretti*, the recurring term *mondo*, literally *world*, means society, preoccupation with earthly things, and the direction of effort principally toward acquisition, possession, power, parade, and pleasure. So when Francis said that he renounced the world, this did not mean, as modern socialists and Marxists generally inter-

pret it, that Francis had turned away from the world and its obligations, and taken refuge in the snail-shell of a secluded life of piety.
The truth is that Francis had, quite literally, renounced society
because he was possessed by the idea of an alternative solution for
overcoming contemporary evils, corruption, the devastation of
wars and social deprivation: the practice of the precepts of the
gospel, following in the footsteps of Christ. This decision, the fruit
of long reflection, meant that Francis did not renounce the world
but fulfilled his life in a different way. The gospel directed him
toward dimensions which had long since vanished from Christianity
as it was then practiced, but in which he saw a way leading to the
salvation of man and the human community.

* * *

"The source and guarantee of freedom for Francis lay in the total
lack of possessions. By virtue of this voluntary poverty a man is
immune to all the usual obligations which life imposes on a society
based on acquisition, possession, riches, and power, leading to
every kind of oppression of man by man. The effect of this hardens
people's hearts, creating fear and mistrust, poisoning the human
community, resulting in rapine and murder, in the tyranny of political and social exploitation, and thus in the betrayal of the divine
image which Francis perceived in every human face.

The total poverty to which he and his companions voluntarily
assented, was not intended as a model for the whole of society,
producing a complete revolution in social conditions. What Francis
wanted was to provide a symbol by preaching poverty and realizing
it in his own person, in order to make people think again and turn
back from corrupt practices. He envisaged rethinking and return
in the early Christian sense as meaning real repentance. When
Francis preached to the masses his aim was to shake them into true
repentance, a change in the direction of their lives. He was absolutely certain that personal inner peace, and still more public
peace, both political and social, could be achieved only when the
fatal lust for power and possessions was denied. He had no desire
to impose the poverty of himself and his companions on anyone
else; it was meant to serve as an illustration that a life guided by
the gospel, and above all the unqualified imitation of Christ, would
bring peace and freedom to the world.

20. St. Francis in Ecstasy by Giovanni Bellini (1426–1516). (The Frick Gallery, New York City.)

• • •

To those inspired by the teaching of Francis of Assisi, a peace guaranteed by atom bombs is unthinkable, the accumulation of wealth and its dissipation on ever-increasing armaments for war is not only a betrayal of Christ but also of the countless millions of human beings, made in God's image, who are the victims of malnutrition, poverty, and hunger. When we remember Francis, born more than eight hundred years ago, there is no question more than his way of penance and his radical conversion, seen in its true historical significance, is a revolution without violence, embracing every area of society, in the name of the Christian gospels.

In Writing this present book, it has not been our primary intention, as we have said, to present a biographical account of Francis of Assisi. **Rather, we** have endeavored to share with the reader something of what we have experienced as the result of our efforts to penetrate into the inner qualities of Francis's *Canticle of the Creatures*.

This effort has ultimately led to our observing the existence of a ninefold path of spiritual enlightenment living within the structure of the canticle itself. As the words of the canticle repeatedly remind us, its prime motivation is to enhance our spiritual faculties of gratitude, thankfulness, and joy, so vitally essential for humanity today. **Truly this** awareness is as imperative now as it was in the age of Francis himself, when the leading human and spiritual motivation was to respond to the signature of that time as expressed in the words "God asks." **In a** triumphant burst of joy, the final words of the canticle ring out to us across the centuries, that this is to be accomplished as we "serve him with great humility."

This can be regarded as a kind of intensification of the words of Christ himself, when he said to his followers: "I have not called you servants, but friends" (John 15); in other words, the essence of the canticle expresses the utterly profound truth that all creation, in reality, is united with the creator in a spirit of friendship and oneness.